Seaso
Empowerment

How Resilience and Hope Can Blossom from Roots of Self Hate

Susanne Taylor

To Lisa,
I hope my story offers you inspiration about whats possible, no matter the odds!
Love Su
xxx

The conversations and events in this book are portrayed to the best of the author's recollections, though they are not written to represent word-for-word transcripts.

Rather, the author has retold them in a way that evokes the feeling and meaning of what was said and, in all instances, the essence of the dialogue is accurate.

All names and identifying details have been changed to protect the privacy of the people involved.

Cover design by: Susanne Taylor

Acknowledgements

This book would not have been possible without the unconditional love and encouragement of my mum, Anne Brislen. You have held me up on the darkest days and always shined light on my branches.

To my children Harmony and Troy, you are my world, the reason I am the woman I am, my motivation for success and the roots that keep me grounded.

You have put up with Mummy getting up at 5am to type for an hour, have been patient and tolerant when I'm tired or grumpy and make me feel beyond proud to be a guiding hand in your lives.

To my fellow author, one of my best friends and my writing den partner Nathalie Reeves-Billing, you have given me the sanctuary to create, listened to endless moans and worries, ran through ideas with me and been both an inspiration and a catalyst for this work.

To my adopted God Dad Roger Axtell, you have remained a rock and foundation for me for over 20 years, checking in on me daily, cheering me on and reminding me how far I have come. I am blessed to have you in my life.

To my dad, whose passing changed my perspective on living and whose memory serves as a reminder how even the deepest wounds can heal. The squirrel in my tree, forever watching over me.

My editor and friend, Clare Coombes, you read through my first scruffy drafts and never told me to give up the dream. Your belief in me gave me the belief in myself.

Minion Portraits for capturing my personality through your amazing photography.

To the readers, friends and family members that are impossible to list.
Thank you for your support and faith in me. It has been invaluable.

Contents

Seeing the Wood for the Trees

I've always felt an affinity with trees. Right from a young age walks in the woods brought me back to a sense of grounded-ness.

Smelling the lingering damp and earthy bark. Seeing the fractures of light beam down through their branches and cross my path, like spotlights looking for the leading act. Sitting with my back against them like grand armchairs whilst eating impromptu picnics. Scrambling over the twisted root systems and peering into the miniature caves created in their trunks. Examining the array of multi-coloured, multi-textured lichen worlds on their bark. Rough and coarse to the touch, yet brittle, and fragile as crystal.

Driving in a tunnel of trees as they wrap their arms around me in a cocoon of safety. Lying under ash trees with the green leaves highlighted and shadowed against each other like a camouflage print, contrasting against the crisp blue sky. Silver birch leaves on a blustery day whispering to each other in hypnotic white noise. The smell of pine transporting me right back to Christmas and the pillowcase at the end of my bed. Anticipation and excitement anchored in aromas.

A place of shelter, of climbing adventures, a resource allowing us to write, create and build. The lungs of our planet and the fruit bearers that feed us. Like sentinels watching the passage of time as centuries pass them by. Witnesses to wars. Survivors of droughts, earthquakes, storms and floods.

Such wisdom and knowledge contained in their stripes of service, as rings around their core. Growing in their unique way, unapologetically and unabashed.

Some trees survive well independently, others thrive as part of a forest in synergy with each other. They all have their value and purpose.

We can learn a lot from trees just by observing them, and for me, there is no better way of watching them evolve than through the different seasons. Acknowledging how the changes may shape their appearance, but don't take away from their beauty or strength.

Spring bringing buds or flowers and hope of warmer days ahead. Summer bringing bouquets of lush green leaves. Autumn, painting cascading leaves with shades of fire and providing crunch under wellies on damp mornings. Winter filled with skeletons waving their arms and fingers in the sky, holly and spruce proudly keeping their coats on and providing an accent of colour in an otherwise barren landscape.

I draw on these seasonal shifts as a reminder for how our own life runs in cycles. How every season has its purpose and time.

There are new beginnings, growth, letting go, challenges pushing us to bend in the wind and asking us to stand tall through it all. We are filled with budding ideas, blossoming careers, branching out to new ventures, yet remaining rooted in our core values and beliefs.

We too can live autonomously or choose to live in harmony with others creating a magical woodland.

This book has been two decades of pondering, germinating and flourishing. Writing has repeatedly been a theme in my life.

Diaries, poetry, pen letters, blogs. I've known that there was a book inside waiting to flourish; I just wasn't sure what that book was going to look like until I stopped trying to see the wood for the trees. Getting caught up in the details instead of allowing the words to land on the page.

So here it begins.

A journey through the seasons of my life so far. From the seed cracked open by circumstance and nurtured to grow, to the seedling seeking light and building strength, right through to the seasoned tree that I am today.

I am not a Mighty Oak. I don’t carry all the wisdom of the forest. I can’t shelter you from every storm. The broken branches you have suffered may never completely heal. You may never love the form that you are in. You may always question your worth. You may continue on paths of self-destruction within relationships, abuse of food, or life choices. But you can find nutrient-rich soil, develop stronger roots, and begin to thrive and bloom. I am a testament of that.

The stories that follow are my experiences in life, what I’ve learned from those experiences, and what I’ve come to accept as part of my evolution. You will travel through narratives of renewal, expansion, releasing, rest and reflection. This will serve to inspire you, stimulate your sense of curiosity and spark conversations in your mind about the pathways you have before you, despite where your old root systems were laid down.

This story is about finding branches of resilience within your own human experience. Reading the journey of an everyday girl, who has risen strongly, and who wants to empower others to do the same.

I’ll encourage you to start seeing the imperfect tree within the wood and admire its unique beauty. For that tree is you.

The Beginning of the End, & Back to the Beginning

Aylesbury Eating Disorders Centre.

I couldn't imagine life ever getting lower than this. I'd been ushered into the room by a small, wide-eyed African lady, Nettie, who beamed a porcelain white smile that contrasted beautifully against her bright blue and purple jumper.

"Get yourself comfortable, dear, they are all lovely here."

I wanted to smile back, but comfort was currently far from capable in my stick insect frame.

Sitting gently and steadily on a quilted patchwork cushion on the squeaky bed, with bones protruding through my rice-paper thin skin. A dripping tap down the hallway, beating louder than my heartbeat. My head was cloudy with a cocktail of fear, desperation and surrender.

There was no smell of home to be found here. Bleach, fabric conditioner and an unfamiliar scent went drifting past my nose in cartoon clouds. Not quite a peppermint smell, not quite Calpol.

I'd later become familiar with the pink liquid sliding down past my dry bulbous tonsils, soothing the burning pain in my chest, but for now, Gaviscon was an alien smell in the air.

I yearned for the scent of my mum's bread baking, a partner's aftershave or a deeply filled bubble bath. Anything that wasn't this hollow cell of my own consequence.

Each movement I made was to be felt in aching bones, funny bones, clickety-clack. Shivering in ten layers of woollen shells, wrapped around the downy hair upon my skin. An armour that had served me well for some time and kept many questions away. But when you start collapsing in the street more and more often, not even an inflatable sumo suit could hide the form beneath. Like the lichen I adored, I was brittle and fragile.

I'm unsure how long I sat there, a young chick in the nest, mouth open wide waiting for mummy bird to return with sustenance. Except there would be no mummy bird coming here. This nest was empty, but for the bed I sat on and a small desk, its ceramic lamp with a flickering light bulb reflecting my own flicker of hope.

The starch white sheets crisp and ironed to within an inch of their lives, trying to bring order to the chaos of my reality, yet failing.

How did you end up here? Emaciated, helpless and dying? A deep sigh.

How are you going to claw your way back? What if it's too late? What if too much damage has been done?

The words resonated through my brain like a pneumatic drill, shattering through ambitions fuselage and bringing floods of tears.

I've never been enough. I'm worthless.

My thoughts an attempt to justify the penance I had inflicted upon myself for all these years, as if there would be some sort of atonement for wanting to step out of my skin and start over.

Winter would be coming soon, and yet here I was in autumn, still with so many things to let go. The tomb of self-hate and self-doubt I had sealed myself in would need to be broken open. I had played the role of victim so well, but there was no Oscar to be presented here, no award for those years of suffering.

'You have to look back to move forward.' Advice that I'd heard with conflicting argument. 'Don't get stuck in your past, look to the future.' Except at that point I couldn't see a future. My body was weak, my mind even weaker. So maybe looking back and trying to understand what led me here was the only option.

To see how the knots were formed, how my branches grew so thin and delicate, how I had allowed poison ivy to creep up my bark and intoxicate my thoughts. I wasn't looking for hindsight, I was looking for insight.

I had to go back to the spring of my life, my childhood, and start to play witness and detective from there.

Spring

New life begins,

The magic of fresh opportunity

Crisp mornings and grass adorned with crystal droplets glistening in the sun

Buds emerge and reach for the light, expanding, growing

Seeking out nourishment and life force energy

The air is clear, bright and promising

Adventure awaits

Lambs bounce, carefree and light, as cotton wool balls
against their vivid emerald carpet

Flowers waving hello as you pass, unashamed of their presence

The outward journey of growth is rapid and intense

Play, dance, creativity and laughter are the theme tune

Paint spots of colour at every turn, like hundreds and thousands
decorating the floor and branches above

The smell of daffodils and crocus tickling your nose

New life begins, again

New Life Begins

My childhood was filled with such mixed emotions. Happy times and struggles. Intertwined like hazel branches into neat little baskets, knotted and broken in places, but a container for the lighter moments bundled inside. A veritable picnic of experience.

I liked our new place in Wallasey. It felt much safer than the unsettling surroundings of our family home in Toxteth. Fear and anxiety ran through our house there, like words through the centre of rock. I didn't really understand the fighting or why we had random people staying at our home some nights. I heard mumbles about firebombing, and people being attacked due to the colour of their skin, but it didn't make sense to me. My friend Sarah had darker skin than me, but she was still lovely, and always let me share her dolls when we went around to play.

It was the first time I even considered that what you look like affects your life, and how people treat you.

It was also the first time I would face separation.

This new home was just for me, my brothers and mum. Our cosy den.

I didn't mind too much at all. I got to sleep in Mum's bed and the comfort of her arms was all the safety I needed. She lined the bed with pillows to protect herself from bruises. I'm a kicker, my brain works in overtime when I sleep, and my dreams are vivid, even now.

"She's been here before," my mum's friends would say. "She's a sensitive little girl, isn't she?" A sponge for the environment I was in. Absorbing all the data, then processing it at night. These days I question whether this is a gift or a damnation. Dreaming of unicorns and rainbows or simple adventures would be nice sometimes.

We didn't have much in our cave at first. We'd left most things behind. Mum must have been in a rush, or only had a few bags, as we slept on a mattress on the floor and the furniture in the front room was mismatched. We fought over who got the comfy chair, but one of my brothers always won. It had an imprint in the shape of a bottom, it was so well-loved.

*

A year on, we revisited our old house. It had been sold to a builder and we needed to go and make sure everything was in order. It was such a surreal feeling, walking back into the carcass of what was once our home.

The hallway was musty, the woodchip wallpaper flaking off the walls. We walked through the rooms we once ran and played in. "Best behaviour when we go in, you three." We stood to attention, never quite knowing what would happen if we didn't follow orders but being complicit regardless.

The tan-brown leather couch sat in the living room with several cigarette burns in the arm, an exhibit in a museum. The little holes a reminder of arguments heard over Dad falling asleep with roll-ups in his hand. "You'll set fire to this house one day!"

Ironically it wasn't him who started the inferno after all. A vandal had thrown a bottle with burning rag through the window when the house stood empty, and vulnerable to attack. My Dad's pride and joy, the bar he built himself in the back-sitting room became shrivelled charcoal, glistening in the light. Like a movie set, still containing charred glasses and empty bottles, unwanted, left behind. They hung there in recognition of how I felt inside sometimes too.

It had felt easy for my dad to move on. I didn't have a concept of what a 'dad' was particularly, but there was still a branch missing from my world and a sense of being forsaken.

He would come to visit and spend a lot of the time drinking cups of tea and telling mum his woes. I just saw him as one of Mum's friends, with a big fuzzy black moustache, that scratched my cheek when he kissed us hello.

He didn't seem to know how to be a parental figure. His idea of interaction would be to try to tickle me repeatedly with his tobacco-stained hands, desperately trying to get me to laugh, but resulting in me having severe stomach cramps, feeling sick and hating him coming anywhere near me.

I would watch his gold St Christopher glint in the sun against his wiry-haired chest and wonder what it symbolised for him. I knew he had loyalties by the fact he always wore it. Unknowingly, I craved for him to have the same loyalties for me.

Over time he stopped visiting as often, later letters exchanged between us would reveal the why, but at the time Mum became the core of my world and that was enough. For a while.

Moving through the empty rooms, stale and cold, I felt even happier to be going back to our Wallasey house. Moving over the water was a fresh start for all of us. Mum no longer had to answer to anyone about how we lived our life. We had moved away from friction and fighting. Like trees, we could carve our roots in the soil from this point forward. Our new life was beginning.

*

We grew up in a time when front doors were left open, kids played rounders in the street and we went to the shop for the elderly neighbour in exchange for a handful of mojo sweets.

Wandering along the beach barefoot to the local parks, swinging on rope swings, and throwing stones at jellyfish. Ice cream would be eaten until it melted down our arms into a sticky mess, hills would be rolled down like tumbleweed, go-karts built out of old pram wheels, with any bits of wood we could find, and fires started with magnifying glasses and old newspaper.

Cups of sugar were borrowed from neighbours, plastic tubs were filled with leaves to become mini-worlds for caterpillars, glow pets sat by the bed in tribes next to fluffy haired trolls, and torches were hidden under the quilt for reading one last chapter after Mum had closed the door.

*

One of our big adventures was to West Kirby on the train. We would take jam sandwiches, fruit, crisps, and a towel to get covered in sand on the beach. I would sit staring at the train seat's patterns of mustard yellow and navy, crisscrossed and making my vision blurry if I looked at them too long. The sound of the train on the tracks; hypnotic and rhythmic. I felt happy there. Melodies of happy memories being stored with every click rolling over the track.

We got off the train and found our sticks. It was a perfect game to run them along the fence to create clanging noises as we went. We had lots of games like that; putting an empty juice carton in the spokes of our bikes to make an engine humming sound, making drums out of pots and pans, or using leaves as whistles. Musical signatures of our days as a family.

"Mine's louder than yours!" We'd fight. Like cubs. Always asserting our place in the pack. I liked feeling part of the pack though, regardless of my status within it. Running ahead of each other and shouting back, "Slow coach, can't catch me!" It would be a lottery of who was going to trip on a kerb first.

Thud! Onto the rock-hard concrete floor. The pain reverberating through my whole body and the shock waves buzzing in my ears. Mum ran to me straight away, scooping me up and bundling me in a swaddle of hugs. Kissing my head and repeating "naughty floor!" while waving her pointed finger at the ground.

She grabbed the pink 'magic cream' from her bag and covered the grit scraped graze with witch hazel.

"Stop! It stings!" I screamed. "It will for a moment, my love, but it will soon be ok." Such soothing tones, lulling me into serene and fluffy clouds of cotton wool comfort. Bringing back the light and carefree notes to accent my day.

All would be right in the world again. Pain is temporary and so are tears.

We continued to the beach and lost hours building sandcastles, paddling and playing. The squelch of the wet sand between our toes, the fragrant sea air, the sound of laughter.

Life seemed so simple. What we lacked in riches we gained in memories. A perfect space to bud and grow.

Fresh Opportunity

Dawn was my best friend. She lived two doors down and was always happy to see me. A few years older, she had long golden hair, a slight frame and funky style. She was everything I wasn't: elegant, musical, confident and athletic. I admired her and wanted to be just like her. We were thick as thieves, two trees that thrived well together.

"Let's make a den and I'll hide here until the morning," I suggested.

Dawn giggled and agreed. So, we set about gathering sheets from the airing cupboard, pegs, a maiden and a few chairs. How we thought it would go unnoticed I don't know, but this was at a time when I thought if I closed my eyes during hide and seek, that no-one could see me.

It took us nearly an hour to construct a masterpiece that even Frank Gehry would be proud of.

We went on to collect supplies of biscuits, teddies, a pillow each and a lamp. All the important things.

"Time for Susie to go!" her mum shouted through from the front room.

"She's already gone home," returned Dawn, in her most serious and plain-faced lie voice. We both burst out laughing. A little bit of mischief felt fun.

Of course, we didn't get away with it. No idea why, and no idea how her mum found us in our invisible hideout. She obviously had bionic vision.

It was a school night and I was reminded, "You're welcome back any time, but right now sleeping in your own bed would be the wiser option."

School was a whole different story, which we'll hear about later, but house number 16 was light relief, and my opportunity to learn how contrasting the world could be.

Even within the darker days, when the canopy above virtually blocks out the sun, there are shards of light reflected from the pools of water upon the floor.

Number 16 was my pool of light.

Dawn's mum became my adopted 'Aunty Joan'. A bubbly lady, with a cheeky laugh and a huge heart. Her hugs were like a warm feather duvet being wrapped around you on a frosty morning. The house smelled of chocolate and unconditional love. We would have treats of cream soda from the pop man and while away hours with 'girl talk'.

It was the perfect escape from two older brothers who loved to torment me. Dawn hated my brothers for that, and I loved Dawn for hating them.

*

We went to the local disco together and she would lend me clothes to wear.

"You can have my black rah-rah skirt if you like? See if it fits?" It went on perfectly, smooth satin against my cool legs. Long, flowing and graceful. I spun round to watch it swirl and felt instantly like a princess.

The room was half empty, rainbows of lights flashing around the walls in the dark from the mirrored silver globe in the centre of the ceiling. The floor felt tacky like it was covered in sap, and tired like worn rope. I wondered how many people had walked across the carpet and lost hours of their evenings on the wooden dance floor.

"What are you wearing, weirdo?" A jibe from the spotty boy over the music in the hall. My heart sank. To go from feeling so beautiful and like a sophisticated panther, to feeling completely deflated and wanting to run home within a split second, was a stab to the chest. The music faded into a dull noise, deadened by sadness. He knew he'd got a reaction and it made his tormenting smirk even bigger.

"Leave her alone, you bully!" Dawn stepped up. My protector. My ally. My best friend. A towering shield in front of me.

Tutting, he backed off, flicking his floppy jet hair off his face. "Pair of weirdos!"

"Just ignore him he's an idiot!" Dawn's tone was motherly and robust. She didn't even flinch when he'd come over. I definitely wanted to be more like her.

The sting was still there, but I didn't feel so alone. I had someone fighting my corner and someone who believed in me. Dawn gave me the chance to grow in a world where I was being suppressed, and her loyalty was never unnoticed.

Emerging and Reaching for the Light

I was budding into life with optimism and had an element of freedom that would not last long past the first decade of exploring. So many times, I'd heard grown-ups say to "enjoy childhood because it's fleeting," but they were words of mystery that had no real substance to them.

Adults had so much more fun; they could do what they liked, and they never had to go to school. There were way too many rules as a child, always things to tidy away and bedtimes to stick to. I was looking forward to being a grown-up and making my own choices, or so I thought.

*

I wasn't one of the cool kids at school. I didn't have the latest clothes, CD players, magazines or computer games. I was never enough.

Ice blue-eyed boy, Jack, with mousey brown-hair, would choose me as his prey and single me out for his daily attack. He was a sly and calculating little boy, who knew exactly when to pounce, and who controlled the crowd better than police with tear gas.

Our school didn't have a uniform, so initially I wore whatever clothes I loved, including a floaty skirt my mum had bought from charity with smarties printed all over it.

"Eeee, look at you! Your skirt looks like me nan's curtains!" The words spat out of his mouth like venom. "It's big enough to be me nan's curtains too!" Bite number two. "I bet you stole them from her house, you scrotty tramp!" Fangs piercing a third time. My heart was dead and out for the count. Pools forming in the corners of my eyes, a pathetic antidote to his poison.

"Aww she's crying, look!" The menacing grin spreading across his face, gathering an audience to the circus freak. The pantomime dame with her frumpy costume. Short, round and fat. A dumpling in the tarmac soup of the playground. Floating alone.

The bell rang and I was saved from the ridicule for another short while. I would never wear that skirt again.

"Mum, please can I have normal clothes like everyone else?"

"Normal clothes? Has something happened?" I couldn't tell her the truth. "No. I just don't like this silly skirt anymore. It doesn't really fit anyway."

She would bag it up for charity once more and I would cry for its fate. That skirt made me feel like a majestic doll. It would puff out when I span around and was softer than silk upon my skin. It made a beautiful whooshing and whirring sound as I moved. Musical, colourful notes. I'm sorry my friend, but you must go.

The sad thought swirled in my head. Individuality would not be tolerated. I was a shy and anxious mouse in a room full of smooth, proud cats, and I would need to toughen up fast if I wasn't to be devoured whole.

*

My hair was cropped short and looked like it had been cut with a bowl on my head (which on one occasion it was), my cheeks rosy and splattered with freckles, using a dirty plastic straw. I was prime cannon fodder.

I quickly learned that it was a time of following the crowd. Building foundations and striving for my branches to begin reaching out for nourishment. Yet knowing there were so many other trees competing for the light that if I didn't keep up, I would be lost in their shadow and crushed in the undergrowth because of my weaknesses.

I knuckled down in class and tried to stay under the radar as much as possible.

I was a teachers' pet and sought comfort in being the most helpful student. One of my favourite teachers was a portly, middle-aged man with a thick, black bushy beard. He always drew smiley faces on my work and had a bellowing laugh that reverberated through the room. I would have loved him to be my dad. A springtime Santa, jovial and welcoming.

In his spare time, he played Sea Shanties, and Mum would take us to watch him in the local park bandstand a few times. Mr Connor didn't judge me on what clothes I wore or how big they were. I was a good kid regardless.

"You're super clever, Susie, and very funny. Why don't you try the drama club after school?"

Drama club? Surely that meant standing up in front of people to be laughed at?

"Erm, I'm not sure that's a great idea, Sir."

"You can be anyone you want on the stage, Susie. You can use your imagination and get lost in a character. I think you'd love it really."

I desperately wanted to trust him. Getting lost for a while did sound good! So did being anyone I wanted.

Fine.

*

The teacher was a tall and gangly woman. She oozed theatrics with her patchwork dungarees, frizzy brown hair that resembled a clown's wig and a perfume of fuzzy peach with strawberry. She spoke with arms waving around as if she was conducting an orchestra. Her tone was melodic and melted away any anxieties within minutes.

I was soon on stage pretending to be a teacher myself and commanding other students to "sit down and settle down!" This did feel good after all. They did what I said, because they were playing a part too. I was in control and powerful for the first time. A strange but alluring feeling.

"You are very good at acting, Susie. Your ability to get into character so easily is a skill. We have a part in a play available with our actors' group, and I'd like to put you forward. It's the leading role of Oliver."

A tennis match went on in my body.

Heart excited and screaming *Yes!* Brain deadpan with a resonating; *Don't be stupid, you'll be ridiculed and booed off the stage!*

Memories of being an angel in Christmas performances, wearing white tights and white t-shirt only to be laughed at by the other kids.

"You look like a flump!" One would start.

"She's the Christmas pudding!" Another would jeer.

"She must have eaten the whole turkey!" The third would throw in.

Not the most inventive or hurtful words, but I was ganged up on, and that hurt enough in itself. I couldn't put myself through that again.

Heart rolling her eyes. *Here we go again! Always with the doom and gloom. This is a great opportunity, Susie. Someone believes in you.*

Brain guffaws. *As if! She feels sorry for you and can't find anyone else. Say no, Susie. Don't put yourself through it. Say no!*

Urgh. Exhausting. These matches could go on for hours if I didn't take their ball away. Two quarrelling teenagers, who both needed to be right and claim their trophy.

"I'd love to, Miss, but I have a family party that day." Wow, now that *was* good acting. Very quick fabrication too. Maybe I was better at this role-playing than I thought.

"That's a shame, but maybe next time, hey?"

Yes, maybe next time.

Brain won the tournament. Heart slumped off. A sore loser. Maybe next time written across the t-shirt on her back.

I never even told Mum I'd been approached. It was an opportunity that wouldn't come around again. A life-changing opportunity. That's the thing about opportunities though. They can only change your life if you accept that you deserve them, and I wasn't worthy of opportunity back then.

*

I remained a loner, a bookworm who got on with her work and retreated into her shell every playtime.

I would save the crying for when I went to bed. Away from the eyes of those who would use it as fuel to attack the fat trampy kid more.

Home was my safe haven. In school I felt like a complete outsider with few real friends, but at home I felt free to just be. The words of blob, freak, hobo, ugly cow, skank, pig, weirdo, witch, scab, somehow melted away.

Seeking out Nourishment

Food was the glue that held our family together.
The cork, in the void of my dad's presence.
The comfort, when pain tried to make an unwanted appearance.

We would have our baking day on Sunday, and it was a sacred affair. I would help my mum with the jobs, licking the spoon as we went, and fulfilling a crucial part.

The kitchen would be filled with aromas of nutmeg, cinnamon and allspice injecting every cell of the air. Pyrex dishes of bread and butter pudding, corned beef hash, syrup tart and cheese and onion quiche. The rice pudding forming bubbles on its surface like blistered domes, popping and reforming.

I never considered that baking day was born out of necessity; it was mine and my mum's little coven. We were on the breadline, and so home-cooked food went a lot further than potato waffles and burgers, but to me, it was a time of great wonder.

At one point my mum returned to night school to try and finish her teaching degree. We would go around to the childminder's house, Debbie, who had porcelain dolls and masks lined up on shelves around her back room. I visualised them coming alive at night long before I watched any horror films.

Debbie was a similar age to my mum but completely different in character. There was no messing about in her house; she never missed a trick. A slight lady who ran on nerves and activity. She would feed us with cheese and ham toasties, and we would read Beano comics until Mum came to collect us.

Then we would go home and cook jacket potatoes in foil on the open fire, coals spitting molten shards at the rug, that you would watch sink into the pile, leaving a tiny black crater in its wake.

I'd climb into bed with my mountain of teddies, that I never had enough of, oblivious to how much my mum must have been struggling to hold everything together. We would "never go hungry, there would always be food on the table!"

Even when money was so short that Mum resorted to making us sugar butties, we saw it as a rare treat. Whilst she probably felt like the world's worst mother providing such a nutrition-less meal, we never felt without, regardless.

She took on several side jobs to keep a roof over our heads and things ticking along. Accounts for friends, newspaper delivery with the old Silver Cross pram and packing plastic eggs for vending machines.

That was one of my favourite jobs she had. I would help her pack the eggs with tiny parachute soldiers, rubber finger monsters and yoyos before bagging them up into bundles of hundreds ready for collection and payment.

We could keep any leftover toys. There were parachute soldiers hung on the phone line outside our bedroom window for many years to come after that.

She also worked in New Brighton fair for a short while, which meant we could get free rides in the holidays. Bumper cars and waltzers, punctuated with fish and chips or candy floss melting on your tongue.

Food was the comma or full stop between every experience.

*

"Why don't we get Easter eggs like everyone else, Mum?"

"Because they're a waste of money!"

I sat pondering that for a minute. There were three boxes of Animal biscuits in the kitchen cupboard where we kept the bowls. I'd seen them when mum was making my porridge half an hour ago and suddenly concocted a plan. It wasn't Easter for two days, but I'm sure no-one would notice if there were a couple of biscuits missing. Baking day had involved apple pie this week. I wasn't a fan, and a bit of chocolate would go down a treat.

All I would need to do was get one of the small stools from the back room, stand on that, and I could probably reach the top shelf. There would be no harm done and my rumbling belly would feel a lot happier.

I waited until after school. Mum was pre-occupied with my brothers fighting each other over who was "the master" and giving each other dead legs. A common occurrence really and the perfect distraction.

I got my wooden podium and began to negotiate my climbing frame. Foot on the bottom shelf, glass framed doors like wings, flapping with every movement of the unstable wooden body, second shelf, nearly there. If I could just reach up...

Crash. I tumbled to the floor, the glass from the doors was in shards around me, bowls and plates buried me in a mound of cloak and dagger.

How are you going to explain this one, Susie? Shut up brain. No-one needs your input here.

Mum stood over me, hysterical. A panoramic view of her child surrounded by glass and blood. I miraculously only had one gash on my arm, but children have a habit of bleeding a lot from the smallest cuts, just to add extra terror into their parent's panic.

"What the Hell happened here?" I couldn't tell if her expression was pure anger or pure fear. Probably both.

Our kitchen was a galley kitchen, so the top of the cupboard was wedged across wall cupboards the other side. An overhanging mass, threatening to crush me beneath.

There was no way I could say it fell; there was no way I could explain the stool, and there was no way I could say I wanted some chocolate because I'd had a horrible week in school.

All I could say was, "I'm sorry, Mum." Guilt sealed into my gut like branding.

That wouldn't be the last time my mum would fear my death. As children, we believe we are invincible. There is little consequence to our actions, and we are blinkered to danger. It's both a blessing and a curse.

*

Food highlighted where there was love, but it also highlighted where there was lack.

My dad was getting remarried, and I was to travel down to Devon with my nan and grandad to be at his wedding.

They bought me a teal green and cream skirt with blouse and waistcoat and white satin 'clip-clop' shoes. I felt a sense of pride and importance. My mum had cut my hair with a fringe and sewn me a Care Bear to take down with me for company. The excitement fizzed inside at my first trip away from home. I would feel part of my dad's world and there would be no void anymore. No missing branch.

How magical.

Although magical it wasn't.

The wedding breakfast came out course by course. Each one another twig being snapped.

Prawn cocktail, the classic starter, except I was sensitive to shellfish, something we'd discovered the day before after trying fresh crab cakes and my mouth tingling and burning. I pushed the bowl aside.

It was ok. I didn't need three courses, two would be plenty.

Steak with fresh cream and peppercorn sauce. I had never eaten steak. Where did it even come from? I cut into it and it was pink and bleeding. It was nothing like the Faggots I'd eaten at home.

"What's the sauce, Nanna? Is it mayonnaise?" I asked.

"It's cream, my sweet." A pause.

"Oh." A second pause. "I can't eat cream because it makes me sick."

Another discovery I'd had when trying strawberries and cream at relatives then spending the afternoon poorly.

"Just scrape it off, dear, you'll be fine."

A third pause. "It's ok, I'll just eat the potatoes. I'm not that hungry." There were two new potatoes, only one of them not infected by the sauce. I ate the solitary spud and two green beans that had made it out clean too.

My stomach groaned in protest. *Feed me!* I told it to stop grumbling. There was still dessert to come.

Chocolate gateau, with fresh cream and strawberry joux.

Crack. Snap. Grumble.

I wanted to be back at home. To be sat in our living room eating fresh bread with marg dipped in homemade lentil soup with fairy cakes for pudding. Anything that had been made with nourishment and love in mind.

Anything that made sense to me. Anything that I could eat without being sick.

It became obvious then; I wasn't part of Dad's world. I was an outsider trying to fit in. That branch would always remain missing and the nourishment I would seek from him would never be fulfilled.

Partway through our stay, I fell off some monkey bars and got a black eye. It summed up how I felt inside. My grandad joked until his last breath how I was his black-eyed Susie, not knowing how symbolic it was for me at the time. I was bruised and broken-hearted.

Bright and Promising

I joined the local swimming club with Dawn and finally found a place where my bulky body frame wasn't a hindrance.

It was strong, powerful and helped me glide through the water, like a hot knife in butter.

My swimming costume transforming me like Superman; from an awkward sea slug into a graceful mermaid.

Suddenly I was weightless, and the deafening noise of life was drowned out into a muffled echo.

The smell of chlorine would transport me straight to one of my happy places, like a zipline through dense dark woods.

I was part of a team. People looked forward to seeing me. They missed me when I wasn't there.

"It's the gala day today, Susie. Have you got everything ready?"

"Of course, Mum!" I'd had things ready the night before. My bag of pride. My bag of purpose. My bag of self-worth and value. Filled with my lucky blue towel, my goggles, my banana yellow swim cap, and the midnight black costume that would be my new skin, transforming me into the body of a winner.

*

The pool stretched out in front of me like a football field, the reverberation of voices around the pool like percussion building momentum.

Deep breath, Susie. Yes, brain.

You can do this! Yes, heart.

The starters gun cracked like a whip and triggered my pounce instantaneously. Diving into the crisp waters, I was a dolphin beneath the blue. Arms paddles in the water and legs my propellers.

Each stroke cut through the words held in my core. "Fat tramp!" Not here. "Useless scab!" Nope. "Waste of space!" Flip turn, pounding feet on the poolside and pushing off the wall with Concorde velocity. Sleek, timeless, flow. Hitting the end of the pool in retaliation, heart still beating in applause.

"Front crawl, silver medal goes to Miss Taylor."

"Butterfly, bronze medal goes to Miss Taylor."

"Backstroke, bronze medal to Miss Taylor."

A beacon beaming, I collected my prizes. I didn't care that they weren't gold trophies. Just the glisten of the metal was enough to shine sunlight back onto my broken branches. Promising my leaves that there were better days ahead. It was safe to bud and grow a little bit. That was all I needed.

I had some direction and focus. There was a sense of achievement injected in my days. We would go on trips to Blackpool, Southport and Wales, fresh adventures and excitement stirred. Wearing our bold yellow swim club tracksuits, unashamed of our presence.

Adventure Awaits

Dawn was at a dancing school and would practise her routines for her shows with natural flair and grace. She would try to teach me moves and we would create our mini productions, performing them in the front room to our mums. An eager audience, always with smiles on their faces, and never bored, despite the repetitive and amateur nature of the affair. The sense of pride in those moments kept me going on more than one occasion.

Her wardrobe was filled with satin flared skirts, tutus with a dozen layers, pristine white tap shoes and royal blue leotards adorned with hundreds of diamantes.

I yearned to be a ballet dancer, wearing beautiful glistening jewels and sheer chiffon dresses, so I asked Mum if I could try a class myself.

"Of course, my love. There's one at the local church hall." This was it. A new adventure. A new branch to grow.

I walked into the vast white hall, with paint peeling in the corner and a pink balloon stuck half-deflated above one of the old wooden beams, watching for any drama, whilst pretending to be helpless and forgotten. The room smelt of furniture polish and prehistoric dust. There was an echo to every footstep and a haze of intimidation.

"I'll pick you up in an hour, ok?"

I nodded reluctantly, a flitter of butterflies whirling in my stomach.

"You will be fine, my love. Try to have some fun yes?"

Deep breath. "Ok, Mum."

There were several girls sat along the tottering benches, pastel pink leotards, with hair scraped back in buns, ballet shoes with ribbons crisscrossed up their ankles.

I looked for a smile. Just one smile to reassure me that I had a place here, but I was transparent as glass and just as breakable.

The teacher arrived with the poise of a swan. Tall, slight and seamless. Her dark brown hair banded with streaks of silver. My mouth went dry, and I could taste apprehension with every gulp. The sound of every swallow being heard by passers-by outside.

She approached me with a staunch look upon her face, eyes up and down like an elevator.

"Susie, yes?"

"Yes, Miss."

"Hmm." Hmm? What did that even mean? Was that even a word? Or was it a sound to snap your dreams in two?

"I'm not sure you've come to the right place, my dear."

Mum had found the class. I'm sure she'd chosen the right one. I wanted to do ballet and all the girls were dressed like the figure in my music box that pirouetted to 'It's a Small World' when you opened the lid.

She must have seen my puzzled look and felt she needed to elaborate further.

"What I mean, my dear, is that I don't think this class is for you. You see we need girls of a certain calibre. Certain standards." The silence in the room now was palpable, only broken by the sneers and whispers of the other girls. A hiss, leaking gas to suffocate me in the room. A deer in the headlights sat stunned, unsure what I was supposed to say.

Obviously, confirmation that she needed to go on. "You are too fat for ballet, dear" There it was. This wasn't another branch snapped; this was someone attacking my core with a chainsaw and leaving me with jagged edges and scars that would never heal. I caught my breath. Choking from humiliation and lack.

I was ten, but light years away from a ten in any judge's eyes. What was I even thinking of coming here? Prancing around your best friends living room was nothing like dancing in a troupe.

Don't you dare cry! Easier said than done, brain. Heart still stunned mute.

I had to get out of there. Mum wasn't back for nearly an hour, but the flush in my cheeks was sepsis spreading throughout my body.

The teacher had been side-tracked by another mum bustling in late, shimmying her delicate seedling into place with the other girls and handing a small brown envelope over for the term's payment.

I scuttled through the side door and headed straight for the toilets. I'd be safe in here until 10.30 and would never have to come back.

Sat in my disinfected bunker, the silver lock with a missing screw and ashen cobwebs above me dancing in irony. Absorbed by the sound of the tap in the limescale stained basin, time dripped away, as I created animal silhouettes from every detail on the cream patterned floor.

Knowing Mum would be five minutes early, I furtively went outside.

"Did you enjoy it?" she inquired; expectant lines etched on her face.

"It was a bit too babyish really. I think I'd like to try something else instead."

Anything but dancing. Yes, brain, anything but dancing.

I couldn't let Mum know what happened. I didn't want her worrying. She had enough on her plate with us three, and I was fine really.

The experience would help me grow thicker bark to protect myself, and it didn't matter that it would stop my creativity from ever truly blossoming.

My roots would have to reach further and deeper than the surface for expressive sustenance and my branches reach higher for inspiration

Play

I had learned how words could leave unseen damage and mildew blemishes, but my spirit still came alive with my imagination. I could rely on that.

I would escape off to lands of giants and swim in their teacups, eating their cake and bouncing on plates of jelly. Worlds where I could be whoever I wanted to be. Princess Laura Daisy, an astronaut, an explorer, a warrior. I would create villages for fairies, leaving them trinkets from my pocket, twigs for them to use as broomsticks and bottle tops for tables.

There was no judgement in my fantasy realms. My inner world was pain-free and magical. There was comfort there. Like the swaddling I had felt in my mum's arms as a baby, it was shielded and could not be penetrated.

I would read books like The Faraway Tree, The Lion the Witch and The Wardrobe and The Borrowers. Each feeding me with the creativity and imagery I needed to build my protective mental maps.

At night my dreams would alternate between flying, weightless and liberated, or night terrors of being stabbed in the back and screaming, but no sound coming out. It reflected the dichotomy of emotions I faced daily.

Happily, lost in daydreams or dying voiceless in the playground.

My solitude brought me a lot of strength. When the weight of life pressed down on me, there was a force inside that pushed me to continue to stand up again. I was in charge of my happiness and could control my internal world, regardless of what I faced externally.

I hadn't quite realised the importance of that resilience yet. The air was still relatively clear, bright and promising. I was still emerging, expanding and growing. I was still able to play, dance and laugh sometimes.

New Life Begins Again

Although I was emotionally tired of being verbally attacked and isolated by my peers, I maintained a carefree and light innocence that was all about to be stripped away layer by layer.

The late 1980s was a time of strange perversity. It may well have been as prevalent before this time, but I distinctly remember my mum telling me "if anyone flashes at you in the park, just point and laugh!"

She went on to explain, "He will be trying to intimidate you, and if you laugh, he won't get the kick he's after." It felt like it was almost seen as an everyday occurrence, accepted as being an inevitability at some point in my life.

I never did see a flasher, but I did experience my first sexually traumatic event at age eleven.

I had played various body discovery games before this point. The whole doctors and nurses, you show me yours and I'll show you mine type scenarios, but I still had no awareness about what the various body parts did, or how they could be abused.

My mum had put an advert in the local paper selling my beloved, but now distinctly clown sized, pink bike. It had rusty stabilisers, a white basket on the front and frayed purple ribbons on the handlebars. When I gripped the hard rubber handlebars, they would leave imprints of small stars in my palms. It was well-loved but ready for a new home.

*

I got home from school and the phone rang. I wouldn't normally answer the phone, but Mum was late, so maybe it was her.

A deep male voice spoke. "I'm interested in the bike. Are there any adults home I could speak to?"

Naive and unaware I replied, "No."

His whole tone shifted. "Hmm." There it was again. That word that isn't a word. A boulder began to swell in my stomach. Something wasn't right.

"I know your mum isn't there because I have her here, with a knife to her throat." The air became stifling, thick with panic and the walls crept in closer.

"I want you to listen carefully to everything I say and do exactly as I ask. If you do as you're told, like a nice little girl, then everything will be ok."

My whole body was dense lead. Beads of sweat formed in the creases of my palms. I was disorientated and my heart pounded out of my chest. My head spun and the fear tasted like metal splinters in my mouth.

"I want you to go to the kitchen and get some vegetable oil and some butter." Shaking, I took the orders and put the receiver back to my ear. "Ok. I've got them." "Now, I want you to take off your underwear and cover your hands in the oil and the butter, then I want to hear you play." This was no frolic for me. "I want to hear the sounds and I want to hear you moan."

The nausea even writing the words still hits me now. The first real experience I had with my own body was as a result of sheer dread about never seeing my mum alive again. To him, it was a game. A kick. A joke. To me, I was stripped of childhood and tainted.

The same butter that had been mixed with sugar and tasted with sneaky fingers when making butterfly cakes.

The same oil that had covered chunky chips served with runny eggs and baked beans. Both now sullied, dirty, bad. Fat was no longer a friend, no longer a treat, no longer a comfort. It was a wolf in sheep's clothing, waiting to turn your sap into resin.

I heard the key in the front door and threw down the phone. Mum opened the vestibule door, confused.

I couldn't find the words to explain what had happened. Somehow, she knew not to ask. Somehow, she knew I felt broken. Somehow, she knew what the phone-call must have been about. She was completely mortified that she had been held up at work and that I had been so brutally manipulated by a stranger we would never be able to trace.

I was left confused by my body's pleasure response, despite the circumstances, and deeply ashamed that I didn't know he was lying to me.

That moment changed how I viewed myself for many more years to come. I didn't trust my body to know right from wrong anymore. It felt like an empty vessel, that I was just a stowaway aboard. Drifting along without a compass.

The ring of the phone triggered a fear reaction for many months to follow. We had to change the handset, so I didn't burst into tears randomly when relatives called. In time life moved on, as it always does.

I buried it. It wasn't a situation or experience I could process yet. I was going to start high school with a different attitude. It was a time of fresh opportunity and I was ready to seek out nourishment, whatever it took.

I was the seedling that had been cracked open, exposed to the dirt of the earth and buried beneath it, but the life force inside continued to glow like Blackpool illuminations flickering in the dark. Tides washed over me, pushing pain deeper to the seabed. They could surface another day.

Flashes of childhood memories still ran through my mind in a flipbook. School trips to the Albert Dock with swarms of ladybirds, not stepping on the cracks on the pavements, and sherbet dib dabs. Falling over on roller skates, trapping fingers in deck chairs, four-leaf clover spotting, and flying kites. Days out catching tadpoles with fishing nets, pebble collecting and daisy chain making. Days on the freshly bleached front yard, making piles of sugar to watch ants' antennae wriggle in delight, or creating necklaces with dry pasta.

Paint marbled memories of beauty and joy interwoven between the sadness and struggle. Constantly flowing.

New life beginning again.

The immature child lost in her imagination and dreams to escape the criticism of the world was entering the season of flames. Her spirit would be both kindled and cauterised. New coping strategies would be learned.

Summer

Evolution continues

The golden torch in the sky smoulders, an intense heat that is hard to escape

The earth filled with nourishment and fertility

Growth intensifies and there is infinite potential in the air

Storms bellowing and lightning cracks

Kids laughter, the chirp of crickets and hedge cutters as the background chorus

The smell of fresh-cut grass drifts past your nose
interlaced with memories and joy

Light rules over dark and the sky is crystal blue, piercing and whole

Vitality, youth, strength, happiness, action, life as an open book

Picnics on verdant carpets and freedom amongst the dance of the sunflowers

Lazy days lying under the protection of trees umbrella,
watching the world go by on a film reel

Dipping your toes in soothing waters with the breeze caressing your cheeks

Vibrant rainbows of roses in a thousand shades, their beauty unhidden

Evolution continues, again

Evolution Continues

Secondary school started with promise. There were so many new faces and there would suddenly be a bit more anonymity for me. I wasn't the fattest or quietest kid anymore and it didn't matter if I had the latest clothes in my wardrobe, because we were all little navy coloured ants, dashing around a huge building, each with our own route to follow.

There was a routine and order to each day, with different lessons, different teachers and the opportunity to immerse myself in learning. I have always had a sense of purpose and value when I've learned something new. I can apply myself to it and watch as my knowledge grows. There is satisfaction in that.

I formed friendships with a select few girls in my class and for the first time, I felt accepted both at school and home. I still wasn't one of the cool kids, but the bullying wasn't as intense and didn't consume me quite as much. There was potential at last.

I became close friends with a tall, slim, girl with soft features and dark blonde hair called Jane. I would stay over at her house and we would buy ridiculous amounts of sweets, stay up until late talking and watching movies on repeat.

"You're so funny, Susie. Can you stay again next week?" Was I funny? Wow. I don't think I'd felt so wanted for a long time. I was still close with Dawn, but she had started high school before me and was already spending more of her time doing homework and going to clubs after school, so we didn't have quite as much space in our timetables for each other.

"I'll ask my mum, yeah!" Maybe I could live there. I loved my mum, but it would be nice not to be tormented by older brothers for a short while.

*

Jane's family were so welcoming and close-knit. I remember watching her sit on her dad's knee with ease, cuddling him and asking him for some cake that her mum had already said no to.

"What did your mum say?" he would ask.

Innocently she replied, "She said to ask you." Her eyes glistening like jewels in a treasure chest.

"Ok then, but it's a treat and you'll have to share it with Susie."

I liked her dad. I liked how he considered me. It dawned on me how much I craved that relationship for myself. That fatherly figure, the protector, the second opinion.

We ate the icing covered masterpiece as if it was the last piece on earth, savouring every tiny mouthful of chocolate goo with our silver teaspoons. Sophisticated dining. It was sweet, dark pleasure, with a hint of vanilla and an after kick of cocoa. A melt in the mouth, melt in the mind kind of cake. Now I knew why Jane worked so hard to get a piece. I would have to remember that skill of manipulation for later. The playing people off against each other, with a hint of deceit, but nothing too damaging.

I had already mastered manipulation at home, sometimes. Getting my brothers into trouble when they picked on me just a little too much, by yelling to Mum to get them told off. For some reason, she nearly always took my side, and so it was a quick pattern to develop. It was either that or join in with the boys and be the honorary tomboy. Play the victim for attention, or put on a mask to fit in. Either worked, depending on my mood.

*

"Shall we go on a bike ride or go shopping?" Jane asked.

I loved both, but the sugar coma of the last 24 hours was kicking in, and I wasn't not sure my legs would have got me up our usual hill on two wheels.

"Let's go shopping!"

Now we said shopping, but we had spent half of our £10 monthly pocket money on sweets the night before, so didn't have a lot left to play with. Not that it would ever stop us. We lived in an era of freedom and youth. It meant we would do one of our usual tricks of trying on several outfits in Tammy and Topshop, knowing we didn't have enough money to even buy one, but feeling like models strutting our stuff in shades of blue, cream and black, chiffon, lace, lycra and denim.

"You look gorgeous in that one. You'll have to save up."

Gorgeous? I didn't think I'd ever been called gorgeous before. It was a little black skater dress, with white detail around the collar and satin floaty skirt. The shape of it gave the illusion of a nipped-in waist, and it reminded me of some of the clothes I used to borrow from Dawn for our dance matinees.

Maybe at some point, I could wear clothes like this for real. Maybe, just maybe, someone else who wasn't my adoring best friend, or my mum, would see me as gorgeous and make me feel special.

Looking down I saw my stomach bulging out of the dress like a quilt stuffed into a pillowcase. *There would be work to do here*, I thought.

Intense Heat

My school days ticked along with lessons of biology, French, English literature and home economics quite happily marching through time. The annoying cuckoo call to my week was simply PE. I may have been a strong swimmer, but my catch was clumsy. I ran like a slug and when I attempted to throw a ball underarm, it would end up behind me. By this point, I was swimming less and less because I preferred weekends with my friends over competitions, so I was more of a sloth than a dolphin.

The changing rooms were cold and oppressive, with nowhere to hide. Made up of a series of benches with coat hangers above them in rows of peeping Tom windows. It was a race to try and get changed under your clothes so that nothing was exposed to be critiqued.

"Eew look at Eve's legs! She hasn't even shaved."

"Have you seen Sally's brown bra. It looks like her Mum's. She must knock herself out with those boulders."

"Beth has been wearing the same knickers for weeks. I bet she's got nits down there!"

That week it was my turn. Katie, the class beauty queen, grabbed my bag and ran around to the other side of the bench before I could catch the strap. I wasn't going to run after her and further play the game of 'trying to get my bag, only to have it pulled out of reach.' I'd played that one enough with my brothers holding teddies out of reach, and I was never a winner at that. So, I had to resign myself to the scene of humiliation that was to follow.

She rummaged through my bag searching for ammunition to fill her rocket launcher. Of course, it didn't take long until her face turned into a contorted snigger and her persona glowed with plasma mockery. She pulled out my navy-blue gym knickers as if they were radioactive waste, only able to be touched with the tips of two fingers and held out at arm's reach with disgust.

"Why have you packed a tent in your bag?"

Of course, now she had the room's attention it was a game of 'join in, or you're next'.

Kerry always loved the joining in. She had a reputation to uphold. Her perfect Barbie figure, manicured nails and chocolate brown sweeping hair, always immaculate. She was untouchable.

“They’re bigger than the school parachute! Maybe you should curl up in them in the gutter, where you belong. You can take some of the cockroaches from the shower to snack on if you like.”

Laughter echoed around the room. Hollow, haunting, harassing and hurtful.

Katie needing to contribute and form allegiance.

“You might as well go, cos no-one wants you on their team anyway. Run home to Mummy and stuff yourself with doughnuts. You’re turning into one already.”

My stomach twisted and lurched. The bark of my face split near the creases of my eyes. Don’t do it, Susie. Don’t even think about crying. My heart was thumping a battle march, but I was already defeated.

*

It would be the only time I was happy to see Mrs Blackford. Her flaxen hair, still styled with a whole can of hairspray into a walnut whip bouffant, bouncing upon her jowly sombre face. The same face that scowled at me for getting a stitch during the torture that was the 1500 metres race and told me to “just run through it”. The same face that would have us playing hockey in all weathers and bark at us to “breathe through the sting” as the puck hit your frozen leg and felt like it was shattering.

“What’s the delay, girls? Netball can’t play itself.”

She looked at me for answers. I hadn’t even got my tie off. I felt panic wash over me. She was going to give me detention.

“Susie, I need you to be captain today. The rest of you had better get your skates on and get dressed, or you’ll be staying behind during lunch.”

I couldn’t believe it. Had someone changed her programming? Why was she being so mild towards me? Whatever it was, it diffused the thrill of the game for the girls, and Katie threw my bag and the navy shorts at my feet. Discarded bullets, dud and bust. Losers like me.

They went on to get dressed and laugh about how many boys they’d snogged that weekend. Oblivious to the damage they’d caused. Like fire raging through the forest until the rain extinguishes it, only to leave scorch marks and embers in its wake. Needing fresh trees to burn next time.

Nourishment and Fertility

The direction of the wind was about to change,
and sunlight would shine on a different part of the forest.
Trees unseen before would be highlighted
and centre stage for a brief time.

I was invited to Cornwall with Jane. Just me, her, and her parents for a week of sun, fun and mischief. An opportunity that couldn't be missed.

I had packed my favourite denim shorts, a few cropped t-shirts and my new violet swimming costume, with palm trees on. Clothes that you would never dream of wearing at home, but that seemed as normal as drinking tea for every occasion when you were away.

The air felt different in Bude, with aromas of freshly caught fish, suntan cream and chips with vinegar. Nothing like our usual West Kirby chips though. These had extra wood notes and a seasoning of sun kissed joy to them.

Everywhere you turned you would be faced with smiles beaming like crowds of glitter balls. It was a town of carefree wonder, kaleidoscopes of bandanas in rustic shop windows, next to waiting lines of surfboards, all trying to get to the front to be seen.

Buskers with long blonde hair played guitars, bongos and didgeridoos, with crowds of dungarees, dreadlocks and butterfly tattoos dancing to the melody. There was a laid-back vibe I had never experienced before. The tension from my defensive facade melted away, like chocolate buttons on a Summer's day.

I felt nourished here, like a new part of me was being conceived. I could be who I wanted to be and get lost in the cobbled streets of festival.

*

"It's beach day!" The excitement from Jane was electric. Static charge pouring out of her being in neon glow. She had been here before, and she fell into the relaxed and chilled atmosphere with picnic blanket comfort.

"What do I wear?" I pondered.

"Anything you want. Wear your shorts and costume. It's going to be scorchio!"

I love it here. Can I stay forever? Anything I want? Foreign language to my ears.

"Here try some of this. It stops you getting as hungry and gives you a flatter stomach."

Jane pushed a bowl in front of me with half of a sliced round fruit on it. Skin orange and tangy, flesh vibrant pink and juicy.

"What is it?"

"It's pink grapefruit. It's good for you. It melts fat away."

Now I liked the sound of that. Fat was a stained word. Tarnished by experience. It brought pain with it like an evil sidekick and I was desperate to start to shake off its blubbery coating.

I took a spoonful, thinking it would taste like orange, and puckering up my face in distorted gurns. Succulent, sour and bitter. Tiny needles piercing my tongue with my brain unsure what to do with the information.

Was this the price of beauty? I had a feeling it was. A little bit of suffering, but a reward of acceptance. *Stick with it.* No pain, no gain, right?

I finished off my half dome. I could see why you wouldn't be hungry for a while afterwards. Mostly because the majority of your taste buds had no feeling left and had waved the white flag in submission.

We packed our bags with giant towels, sunglasses, Sweet Valley High books and coconut face spritzers. A day of basking and freckle collecting ahead. True food for the soul and calorie-free.

That week brought me home a couple of pounds lighter, a few shades darker, with a Cheshire cat smile that left my face aching.

*

We returned to school, but something changed. Suddenly I was noticed. Not just noticed, but admired, by one of the cool boys. I assumed it was a joke and brushed it off. I didn't understand the whole genuine attraction game at this point. My experience was limited to overheard conversations in the playground.

He was persistent though, and I was flattered. It didn't take long to get swept up in the fiesta and frenzy of positive attention I was attracting for the first time in my life and the feeling of fertility coursing through my veins. A dangerous cocktail yet to be tasted.

Growth Intensifies

It took several weeks for Adam to convince me that he really did like me and for us to spend time together. He was a lot more emotionally mature than me, in many ways. One of the tallest boys in the school, a basketball player, and a peacock's confidence attracting everyone's regard. He had hands forged in iron and a smile chiselled out of stone. His presence was impossible to ignore.

Adam had 'life experience' and had already been out with several older women at this point. I'm pretty sure they shaped what he thought was normal behaviour in a relationship, but who was I to complain? This was my first relationship full stop, and I didn't have a benchmark to compare it to, so I should be grateful, shouldn't I?

Suck it up and do your duty.

I had played the role of *innocence*, the role of *teacher's pet*, the role of *model daughter*, the role of *loyal friend*. Now it was time to be the *people pleaser.*

*

"You're funny and cute. Just be careful how fast you turn your head, cos people will have to duck so you don't knock them out with your conk."

I laughed nervously. I was sure it was all just friendly banter, the same as my brothers did. He would joke about things then pull me in for a kiss to soothe away any upset. The after sun to the burn.

"Wow, your chest is like two fried eggs. You might grow into them at some point though, don't worry."

"Man, your bum is big. I think it has its own postcode. Look at it shake when I wobble it."

A jiggle of my flesh, then another shower of affection. It was fine. I shouldn't make a fuss really. Someone who I had looked up to as being one of the popular boys was spending time with me, and I would do anything to hold onto that, to keep that feeling of respect and importance from the other girls in school at last. I had a place in the pack.

Adam spent time with me while I babysat a friend's daughter. We would get a cheap bottle of wine and water it down with pure orange juice. Our own Bucks Fizz. I had already tried cans of lager in the park and diluted it with blackcurrant, so we knew that we could make alcohol semi palatable. It was our way of feeling more grown-up, of being refined, of letting go of the boring school week.

We fooled around on the couch. He taught me things, and I felt like I was accepted and loved. I was his diligent student, willing to learn, gold stars and smiley faces galore.

This would my first introduction to 'poppers'. A lesson in nausea, head rushes and lost inhibition.

"What's that smell? It smells like sweaty feet!" I winced.

"Don't worry, I accidentally spilt some stuff on my top, but it's ok, it will help you relax."

Whilst he had already encouraged me to do things to please him and to stop him 'getting pain in his balls,' this was the first time he tried to do things to me. It was uncomfortable and reminded me of the phone call I'd had those years before.

"What's the matter?"

"I've got stomach pains today and feel a bit woozy. I think it's the wine. Let's watch the movie."

He stopped, the disappointment on his face etched like carved maple. My mind spun from the solvents in the air. *I did feel woozy.*

What was wrong with me? I was messing this up. All he was trying to do was make me happy. I tried to nestle into him but there was a coldness to his hold. The soft embrace splintered with rejection.

The film became the drone, buzzing in our ears. The distraction from the elephant in the room. That time.

*

A few weeks later we were alone together again. Adam was looking after someone's house and invited me around. He reassured me and I felt safe in his company. We watched films and chilled out on the bed, wrapped around each other like curled up rose petals.

We got lost in each other and there was a tenderness in his arms again. The splinters had been filed away and the atmosphere was balmy and languorous.

At some point in the bubble of purity, things crossed a line. A line I hadn't even realised was there until the bubble had been popped.

Sex education in school was limited to watching a video on childbirth, talking about sexually transmitted diseases and the importance of using condoms. There was no discussion about boundaries, love, pleasure, respect, care or connection.

So, it was just an act, right? An act of getting on with it, regardless of how painful it might be or how it took you outside of your body, of how it left you feeling hollow, tainted and dirty, with fungi of shame on your skin that could never be washed off.

It hurt. A lot. I wasn't ready. I wasn't prepared. My mind was a blur of confusion. I needed to be validated, to do whatever it took, I couldn't be a frigid prude.

Just go with the flow, it will be over soon. Yes, brain. It's been a while, but I'm glad to have you here. Heart once again crying and rocking in the corner.

You brought this on yourself. Your desperation for love. Now you must suffer the consequences.

Time dissolved away with the shadows. I left that room a different girl. Treacle bound upon every pore. Tarred and feathered.

If this is what being a woman was, then I didn't want it. I didn't want to go through pain to feel adored, but the cycle had begun. A catalyst had been triggered, and it would be a battle of forces from this point forward.

Growth was intensifying and it felt out of my control. A bush fire raging through my body. Memories of joy shapeshifting between the feelings of prickly heat, blazing inside my core.

Tormented, confused, lost and wanting to escape me.

You're a stupid little girl, really aren't you? As if you could fit in with the lions when you're just a scruffy alley cat.

I went home, battered tail between my legs.

People pleasing meant being left in pain.

Storms Bellow

I had to go to the local clinic for teenagers who wanted sexual advice. I didn't give in many details, just enough to get the chalk-white pills that would ensure I couldn't get pregnant from my discrepancy. Erasing the mistake, leaving only indentations behind on the paper.

There was no judgement, but I still felt ashamed and stupid. I 'should have known better'. I 'should have said no'. I 'should have had more self-respect'.

Except I didn't, and that was exactly the problem. I didn't respect myself at all. It didn't matter how many times my mum told me she loved me, that I was beautiful, that I was amazing. She was my mum and she was 'supposed' to think that. I needed more validation than a doting parent. I couldn't give it to myself. I needed it from others and that was a fatal need to have.

Things in school shifted. Stories were travelling around about me. Certain people I could no longer face. I had to find a way out. I had to find someone to love me again and to take away those feelings of shame, loneliness and self-hate.

By this point, I was already beginning to diet on a larger scale. I switched my usual chips, with cheese and gravy for fruit. People noticed me losing weight and complimented me. It felt good to have some positive recognition woven amongst the criticism and rumours.

I started to go to nightclubs with my friend Louise. The skirts got shorter, and I took more risks getting into strangers' cars. It didn't take long to meet someone who would be my next obsession. He was six years older. A man. A potential protector.

Except he wasn't going to play the role expected of him. There were conditions on our relationship. He wasn't content with cuddles. I knew the drill this time though and was prepared for what was to come.

I quickly learned to escape in my mind. I'd done it before, and I could do it again. I felt of worth and loved in some way. It didn't matter if it wasn't what I wanted. I felt needed and *I* would play the role expected of *me* at least.

The *people pleaser* character hadn't quite worked, now it was time to try the *good little girl* act.

The problem with a relationship as a child, with a man seeking a child, is that there will always be a younger model and that it is always temporary. Which it was.

My heart a kettlebell, beating against the walls of my chest, when he told me it was over.

"You can't leave me. I stayed off school for you. I spent less time with friends for you. I nearly died for you!"

The dramatics were all there. I should have gone for the part of Oliver after all. He had been my rescuer and I couldn't see a life without him. I had taken risks for him and the visions came flashing back like lightning.

*

"Watch this cool move!" he'd said, showing off his hand brake turn skills, on the ice skinned road.

We pirouetted in slow motion, a graceless tornado, with a bus stop edging closer to my line of vision. A roller coaster ride, where my seatbelt had not been put on properly, and one that would end with me in hospital with serious concussion and whiplash. A doctor's record of my naivety and pure luck. The bus stop had caused the front end of the car to fold like a silent concertina, but somehow the force was absorbed enough for me to come out of it relatively unscathed. If I hadn't had such a bulky school bag on my lap, acting as an improvised airbag then I could have been projected out of the windscreen like ammo from a pea shooter.

As he ended our relationship, I wished I hadn't come out of his car alive.

"I'll kill myself without you." Quivering desperation in my voice. My sense of stability and normality broken eggshells, with yolk and white oozing out in protest.

"You'll be fine. You'll meet someone else. See you around, yeah?"

He closed his front door. The blood-red drawbridge had been pulled up and I was no longer welcome to cross the moat. The same front door that had welcomed me in with puppy dog affection for months before and had me skipping as I left, was bolted and chained to keep the vagrants out. The thud as it slammed shut, pounded in my brain like a sledgehammer. The welcome mat on the step laughing at me in mockery and curling up to hide its message.

I was empty.

I had to numb the pain.

I would sit with a needle and carve lines in my arm. I would scald myself under the hot tap or hit my thigh with anything heavy I could find. The destructive distraction that couldn't be ignored. Hours would be lost until sleep came. Days would blur into weeks.

The rumble of thunder in my concave stomach, booming for food.

You don't deserve food. You don't deserve love. You don't deserve life.

Good girls would never be good enough.

Light Rules over Dark

My body was weak and my immune system low. Sweat poured off me like raindrops on a polished windscreen. My throat filled with thorns and my neck swollen like a toad. My appetite had dropped and trying to swallow became an Olympic sport that I wasn't even passing the trial runs for. An apple, a banana and a cup of hot Vimto was all I could manage each day.

The GP examined my ears and throat with interrogation torchlight, took my blood pressure, and stunned me into movement with his ice-cold stethoscope against my damp hot flesh.

"How long have you had the sore throat and fluctuating temperature?" His small brown eyes assessing me with wonder, like a Monet in an art gallery.

"Just over three weeks this time," my mum replied. My translator, dictating in replacement for my pathetic husky croak. "She's had tonsillitis and anti-biotics three times already this year. Surely it's not that again?"

"We need to run some blood tests, but I suspect it may well be glandular fever." He slid his stethoscope back in his desk drawer and pulled out a pen. Clicking it to a point with precision reflexes and signing a blood form for me to take to the hospital.

"Glandular fever? The kissing disease? Will she need to remain off school then?" I had already had weeks off at a time and the school were getting concerned about me falling behind, so I had dropped several of my GCSEs to focus on the five main subjects they felt were important. This was exam year. This was when you got your grades to prove your worth.

They were in the process of providing a tutor to come out to me at home for a few hours a week in the interim period of me returning to school, not knowing that the interim period was going to last the duration of the school year.

My blood tests came back positive. Normally glandular fever would pass, and life would resume on its merry way after a few weeks of rest, but I was already entrenched in dieting, over-exercising and pushing myself to study harder.

My achievements at school were some of the only rays of sunshine I had seen on the dense forest floor, and I wasn't willing to lose my A-star status without a fight. So, the battle of wills between my body telling me to stop, and me going through every red light with sirens blazing behind me, was on. My recovery would have to wait and choke in the dust from my tyres.

It was a relief to be safe in the confines of the home. I was cut off from outside stress and given a complimentary pass to avoid the judgement from other classmates. This was my 'get out of jail free' card and what a reprieve it was.

My body was shrinking back to the childlike girl that came before any sexual violation and my periods that had proved so problematic and painful had stopped. There was a strange satisfaction in that. Maybe I could reset events and start over after all.

*

The side effects of slimming down aren't just your thighs and stomach muscles being deprived of energy, dissolving like sugar cubes when you look in the mirror though. My heart, my lungs and my brain were also muscles being starved.

I struggled to get dressed, get washed or concentrate for long periods. I was running on adrenaline and ignoring the signs of malnutrition. Passing out in the street was a regular occurrence. From both exhaustion, and from my legs giving way with sheer fatigue. My heart was too weak to pump the blood around my body, and my blood pressure would dip to the point of me fainting.

I lost all self-respect, body dysmorphia kicked in, and so did the depression and panic attacks. I couldn't get on buses or trains, get in lifts, be in large crowds or face friends. Isolation was becoming my new norm.

Leaving the house meant carrying a cloak of chainmail that would suffocate me at will. Squeezing my chest like a lemon, extracting all my confidence and leaving me in a heap on the pavement. Noises, a nightclub in my ears, full volume, deafening. Pounding through my brain. Life passed me by like time-lapse photography. I was an observer, not a partaker.

*

My mum was taken into hospital for multiple blood transfusions that year, due to heavy bleeding, so I was able to slip under the radar for a time, baking constantly for my brothers and saying how I'd already eaten. Playing the role of a mother this time, to distract from being the martyr. Coping alone and making the most of my isolated anonymity.

The pressure of exams was creeping up, like a predator ready to pounce. Revision began to weigh heavy on me, overwhelming and constant. I needed to do something. The walls of the cave were starting to crumble, and I was getting blocked in, unable to escape.

I sat with a notepad. Innocent, colourless, clean and pure before me. Its pages rough and exposed to the touch, patiently waiting for my words of invalidation to be tattooed upon its skin.

'I'm sorry. This is too hard, and I can't do this anymore. I love you. I'm sorry.'

I had gathered together a collection of pills like candy in a bowl. A cocktail of whatever I could find in the house. Namely painkillers, anti-inflammatories and vitamins. This was not a well-planned out move, but an act of sheer despair. Tears pouring from my eyes like a monsoon. All hope washed away with drain water.

I don't know how many tablets I managed to swallow before my eyes became too heavy for lintels to hold up and my brother's girlfriend found me and rushed me to the hospital in a haze.

I'll never forget the emetic I was given. I thought my insides were being forced out with the brown ipecac syrup, as it triggered convulsions throughout each cell. I felt stripped clean. Every part of me trembled with fatigue and relief, but a cloud still hung over my head, dark and heavy.

There were doctors and therapists, strangers gathered around, like iron filings to a magnet, all asking me questions about my state of mind.

"What led you to try to take your own life?"

"Would you do it again?"

"Do you feel safe to go home?"

Etheric questions that didn't make sense to me. I was still stunned from the experience and still wanted a way out.

"No, I don't feel safe to go home." I didn't want to be alone with my fears again, but I didn't feel safe in people's company either.

If I'd known the chain reaction my answer would start, then maybe I would have considered my response more wisely. Unfortunately though, it was already settled that I would have to go into an 'institution for adolescents with mental health needs,' and I would be under constant observation and analysis.

The strange beast that was me. An enigma to watch and critique. A freak in a circus. The main act.

My mum would have to gather up some belongings for me and accompany me from the hospital to Chester the next day.

As we approached the dark wooden doors of the centre, black window frames shut-in arbitration, unyielding and suffocating against the lifeless bleached walls of unsympathetic monotony, sheer dread swept over me like no other panic attack I'd experienced previously. A shroud over my lifeless body. Even the pine trees surrounding the building quivered in fear and shuffled uncomfortably in their concrete seats.

A vixen's scream wailed from my lungs and my arms flailed like seaweed in the crash of waves, as the staff tried to pull me away from Mum. I became a banshee, possessed and erratic. Both of us hysterical and inconsolable.

I had no idea if, or when, I would see her again, no idea how long I would be kept locked away in unfamiliar surroundings, no idea what lay behind those doors. Terror ran through my veins like liquid mercury. Images I'd constructed from stories of being taken away from her at birth when she'd needed medical attention, strobed in my vision.

It took three members of staff to prize me away and sedate me into submission.

"This is for your own good."

"You will see your mother soon."

"Behaviour like this is not acceptable and will prolong your stay."

That was the clincher. The good cop, bad cop routine could finish there. The thought of staying even one night longer than I had to was worse than the thought of letting my mum go, so I surrendered. I was spent. Broken and alone. Truly alone. The 52-blue whale, the Lonesome George Tortoise, the Ténéré Tree.

I had to start figuring out a plan. Being stuck in victim mode was no longer going to serve me and something had to change, but I didn't know where to start.

*

The staff in the centre were far from the prison warden stereotypes I had created in my mind for them. They listened to my words of self-hate, without judgement, and gave me a sense of sanctuary. Days had their routines of mealtimes, group counselling, individual therapies and wind down time. We were expected to plan our shopping lists, delegate house duties to each other and become interdependent.

They had diagnosed me with anorexia nervosa, as well as depression and anxiety, but their treatment programme was targeted. I felt truly heard and that was powerful.

The antipathy I'd gone in with started to subside and something was triggered in me.

A fire inside that had laid dormant was beginning to burn harder. An inner sun bursting to get out. I couldn't give in to the dark anymore and there was strength there, waiting to be nurtured, courage waiting to be revitalised.

I sat in my magnolia capsule, with its wooden creaky bed, positive quotes framed on the wall and rainbows cast from the gilded window, and I decided that I mattered. There was more to life than this. I wanted to go home.

"I think I'm ready to leave."

The elfin therapist swept her silken blonde hair behind her ear and adjusted her glasses on her nose. "I see. So, what is different now than when you came to us four weeks ago?"

I wasn't expecting the Spanish inquisition.

Come on, brain, what's different now? Brain was hungover from the overconsumption of art therapy earlier in the day. Teresa stared expectantly at me.

"Erm, well I know I have a purpose now, and I feel like I am looking after myself by eating a lot better."

Do you? Wow heart, I thought you'd ran away with sense of humour. Nice to have you turn up, fashionably late, but appreciated none the less.

"That's really good to hear, Susanne. I will speak to my colleagues and we will discuss possible options moving forward."

My fate lay in the hands of the members of staff. I had followed the programme. I was eating regular meals, and there were no more suicidal thoughts, no more self-harm. I hoped that I said all the right things, but it was out of my control again now.

I lay awake most of the night, staring up at the Artex ceiling and praying that it would be the last time I'd see its valleys and peaks formed into plaster meringues.

I was ushered into the office again the next morning, still yawning from the restless hours of contemplation, listening to the tick of the clock in my room playing metronome to my anxious lament. A panel of three faced me in their settlement thrones. Judge, jury and executioner.

Heart was far from absent this time. Beating her drum wildly in anticipation. Brain whizzing around on roller skates, without brakes.

"We have agreed that we feel you can return to Wallasey with staggered support. Your mum has sourced further counselling with the eating disorders clinic in Liverpool and we are happy with your commitment to your mental wellbeing."

As the words entered the room, like unexpected celebrities at a school theatre production, the sun simultaneously burst through the window, casting light on the dust, dancing in celebration. Heart beat her drum even louder, and brain joined in with a fanfare on his trumpet.

Someone had faith in me. I still didn't know how to change, but I had to at least try. This was the sunrise after the darkest night. This was my chance to shine.

Life as an Open Book

My counsellor was a small buxom lady with the resemblance of a wise old owl.

As soon as I entered her freshly scented room, with its mismatched armchairs, soft luscious cushions and ornate orchids standing guard on the bookshelves, I felt at ease. She was the village elder; whose tepee was a place of refuge and sanctuary. There was a soft melody coming from speakers in the corner, meditative music to soothe the soul. The background chorus with her gentle voice as an accompaniment.

"Come in and sit down. Make yourself comfortable. My name is Rose."

Of course, it was. There could be no other name for someone who emanated love so effortlessly and whose whole demeanour was one of warmth and humility. If I was to pick a colour for her, she would be a lavender rose. Sweet, gracious and regal, with an aroma that was sure to reassure and relax the most skittish in temperament.

I burrowed into the chair, with a cushion across my knee like a lap dog. A plush solace to stroke and cuddle, distracting nervous twitches of apprehension. Settling in for the duration of the course.

"We have a lot of work to do, but I know that you will get there. We will help you build a healthy relationship with food again, and you will learn that there are no such things as bad foods."

She explained that once I'd completed a week's food diary, detailing what I'd eaten and my feelings before and after the foods, that we would then take small steps to introduce a wider range of things back into my diet. That was the easy part.

"The hard part will be facing the reasons behind your need to control what goes into your body. Restricting foods is an outward symptom of inner trauma, and it's that trauma that you are going to have to resolve, for the need of an eating disorder to no longer exist."

That made sense. The food I allowed myself was under my command. I couldn't control the world around me, but I could govern what passed my lips.

"There are a few things we need to do first though. Deeper work will come in time, but right now I want you to regain a sense of achievement and sit your exams. I don't want you to worry one bit about your results.

I left school with no qualifications, and yet here I am today sat with you, helping support young girls through such difficult times in their lives."

The affection in her voice like birdsong, lifting the duvet that smothered you in morning heat.

"It doesn't matter what bits of paper are in your record of achievement, it matters what you are passionate about, and how hard you work to become what you want. It's about seeing things through that you have started, regardless of the outcome. I believe in you and I want you to begin to believe in you too."

*

Her words would stick with me for many years to come. A positive voice and cheerleader in an otherwise critical mind. I took her advice and booked to sit my exams at the hospital school campus.

It was a strange environment. There were other kids there who had been expelled or had various emotional difficulties. Louise, my old classmate and partner in crime on our many drinking escapades, was also there and I was completely caught off guard with how she would react to seeing me.

Schools were full of rumours. I remember hearing that some of the students in school had thought I was in a coma after the car crash I'd had. The rumour that circulated about Louise though was said to have been started by me, and she was about to give me her full thanks.

"Why did you tell everyone I was pregnant? You stupid, fat cow!"

She came at me fiercely and growling, a wolf pouncing on its prey, no reasoning to be had. She screamed at me, grabbed my hair and swung me around like a ragdoll. The whole scene was a blur. I had no time to focus or plead my case; I had to get away somehow.

Mentally I detached from my body. It wasn't me being spun like a discus. There was a disconnect and I was watching the scene through a two-way mirror. Witnessing the event, whilst living it. Her teeth snarled up like a rottweiler, wanting to tear me apart and release all her rage on my limp, pathetic body.

The ordeal lasted minutes yet felt both like seconds and hours. Somehow, she lost her grip and I fled. A bounding deer, running for its life and not looking back.

I didn't stop until I was in the local paper shop, panting, a scrunched-up tremor of adrenaline in the aisles, catching my elusive breath.

It wasn't going to be the last time I would face physical violence, but right then something had been singed away in me. I wasn't quite so fearful of it. I could disengage from my body and the pain would be inflicted on someone intangible, not me.

I'm not sure that was a good skill to have found, because on occasion it made me more accepting of abuse, but regardless, it was useful for more than one battering. I had learned to unlink the chains of suffering and discovered how to disassociate.

*

It was only a matter of days before I would sit my exams. I never saw Louise again during that time. It was another secret I would keep to myself. Another event that would silently shape me with bonsai finesse, no-one needed to know the pruning that had gone into the final form.

I was determined to keep looking forward. To hold onto Rose's words of inspiration. To begin a new chapter and live my life as an open book.

Completing my school year, despite all the upheaval I'd faced, was the opening introduction to the main character. There was a whole story to be written from there.

Dipping Your Toes in Soothing Waters

I continued with the therapy, and we spoke of the bullying, the sexual abuse, the feelings of being isolated and alone.

We also spoke of my dad and how I'd felt unwanted. I'd pieced together broken conversations family had talked about; mentioning how he had wanted to travel around Germany with his friend, how children felt like a burden, and how he had never got over the upset of my sister's death ten years before I was born.

Maybe I reminded him of what he had lost in that child. Perhaps I brought up emotions that were too overwhelming to process. I got it, but the pain of rejection still ran deep. Glowing embers in my bones.

With encouragement from Rose, I would draft him a letter. I had already got used to writing pen letters. Some to friends who were concerned when I left school, some from strangers I'd connected with via pen friend groups and some from family.

I loved to write, and I loved to receive letters in return. That little rectangular timepiece falling through the letterbox with graceful magic, a snapshot of someone's day, scribed in liquid emotion. The sound of the envelope tearing as you opened it, anticipating the portrait in print with a soft crashing wave as it ripped. The smell of the ink and the writer's perfume sealed in their cave until the moment of reveal. Never sure what you were going to find, but always happy to curl up and read.

This was going to be different.

I had written to Dad a few times and visited him a handful of times since he moved to Runcorn with his new partner and soon to be fiancé, Liz. Liz was a powerful character, who was never afraid to speak her mind, no matter how awkward that left the atmosphere on occasion. I admired her brazen nature and she softened my dad somehow.

She pushed him to try and build a relationship with me and my brothers. Partly because she hadn't had children herself, and partly because she knew he was missing out on opportunities to develop a paternal connection. Our letters had always been a matter of fact, see you soon, superficial. So, this would be completely unexpected from me, and I had no idea how he would receive it.

It wasn't received well. I was angry. I was hurt. I tried to form the letter without attacking him, but the words came out like a battering ram. How I knew I wasn't wanted, how I had tried to commit suicide because of the emptiness I felt inside, how he wasn't there for me when I needed him, how he didn't protect me. I was blaming him for all the experiences I'd been through and all the resentment poured out of me in an eruption of lava.

His letter in return felt cutting and cold.

Dear Susie,

It has taken me several days and a lot of thought to try and write this letter. On what to say, and how to say it. I'm sorry I hurt you. It was a heavy lesson wasn't it, to learn that your family have forgotten you? It wasn't only this year I've been forgotten. Your aunt has told me how your mum needs to remind you when my birthday is each year. Even in your own letter, you couldn't say you were sorry for forgetting me.

I know you haven't been in the best of health, but you haven't been dying in a sickbed for the last year, so it's not just effort lacking on my part is it? Are you sure your anger isn't because you feel guilty for not bothering with me? It seems like your interest in me only happens when it suits you.

You say that I never wanted you, but what do you know about life? As you get older you might understand, your mother forgot to take her pill, and although I had no choice in the matter it didn't mean I didn't want to love you when you were here.

When I came to visit, you and your brothers would disappear off to your rooms and I would be left chatting to your mum. It was you I came to see, not her, but I clearly wasn't that important to you.

I know this isn't the letter you will have wanted, but even though I know I haven't been the best dad in the world I have always tried to be there for you all, even when you have pushed me away.

It wasn't my choice to leave, but I do know it was the right choice.

This has been a hard letter for me to write, but I hope that we can communicate better and put things right in the future.

All my Love,

Dad

I never saw any of his compassionate words. I was blinded by the upset of his counterattack and briefly descended into an emotional downward spiral again, the feeling of rejection branded in my mind. Defensive and bitter as lime.

It would be a while before I would respond in return. He was *supposed* to apologise profusely, whisk me up in his safeguarding arms and melt away the years of hurt. I needed him to be stronger than he was. I needed him to be something he wasn't. I needed him to pull the sword from the stone and rectify the wars that I felt inside, but he couldn't.

I had tried to paddle in healing waters, only to cut my feet on broken shells of patriarchy.

*

By this point, my brothers had both moved out of our family home, and my mum had met a partner and moved in with him too. After over a decade of knowing her alone, it was a strange and uncomfortable change. I hated him instantly, without knowing anything about him. This would be the third time that I was separated from my mum, and this time I knew it would be permanent. I didn't like that concept one bit.

Looking back now I was a selfish brat, terrified of what it meant to be on my own. Being in my own company hadn't been a positive thing for a long while. At the time all I could see was abandonment, betrayal and indignation. My mum was finally living a life that would make her happy, and it was the best thing she could have done.

I didn't have a choice in the situation. She was leaving the nest I had got too comfortable in, and it was about time I figured out how to fly solo. She was moving in with her partner and our co-dependency would have to be severed. I was left in the home that we had grown up in, but there was no family there anymore. As brutal as it felt going through it, I would have to try dipping my toes in the water of life again.

*

It took months before I accepted her partner enough to visit them. Years to accept him enough to be happy for them.

He was a completely different generation to me, ex-army, and I didn't understand his dry or crude sense of humour. His masculinity threatened me, and I was on edge being around him. He was the magpie that had come down and stolen the maternal egg that was providing me with sustenance.

I didn't see how much he loved my mum, how big his heart was or how much he had suffered in his own life with previous relationships, intoxicated by alcoholic and abusive partners.

We all have burning coals we have had to cross. Sadly, I didn't acknowledge his fire walk sooner, because he played such a positive father figure in the years after I let my guard down.

Within months I had lost the fantasy of building a relationship with my dad, as well as losing the relationship as I knew it with Mum. I was sensing a recurring theme with this isolation lark.

My determination spurring me on through it all. Even when the grass grew so tall I could no longer see a path to tread, I would continue to put one foot in front of the other.

Things weren't all dark and difficult during my days. I was working part-time with my mum in her office job and had returned to school to do my A levels. A feisty spirit inside kept me moving forward and trying to find a better life. Pacing the steppingstones across the river of rapids trying to draw me in, I was able to get my feet wet without being pulled under again.

I might survive alone. I might make it to the other side of the stream.

Rainbows of Roses

I was going out most weekends with my brother to rock clubs. I dabbled with smoking weed and one night took acid. It was not a good experience for me. The darkness of my mind was exposed in vivid colour. Walking through arms grabbing at me in the nightclub, watching the walls stretch and tower above me until I was sat on the floor in a foetal position, afraid of what I might see next.

It was enough to turn me away from any further drugs. I already saw the freaky faces people pulled on speed and heard the stories about heart attacks on ecstasy, so that was all I needed to know to be terrified of taking them myself. Alcohol would be my drug of choice. Socially acceptable and without the negative press. The mind justifies things in such strange ways.

*

I met a new group of friends. One of them became one of my closest friends to date, James. I could talk to him about anything. He knew my history, about my struggles, and yet he accepted me regardless. He was there for me at a time when I felt so desolate, that he became my world. We spent nearly every moment we could together. I felt part of his family and so at home with him. He had two sisters, one older and one younger. I had always wanted sisters, and they welcomed me into their life with open arms.

His mum was a strong, vivacious character who loved to make sure her children were well fed. There were always roast dinners, cakes and chocolate in the house. A binge eaters Heaven and Hell rolled into one. She was separated from his dad, but they still shared the house. He had his room he would spend time in, and they would only pass in the kitchen. I admired how they made it work, despite clearly resenting each other.

I wondered what it would have been like to have my dad live with us when his relationship with Mum had broken down. It allowed James and his sisters to have a relationship with their father without being passed around like parcels at the weekends, so I guess in some ways it made sense. James accepted it as his norm regardless.

*

We would go to gigs together, festivals, weekly cinema trips, on holidays and have Christmas with his family. I felt part of something, I felt loved, I was truly cared for. Things were good, for a while.

"Are you ok? You seem very quiet." James's head tilted to the side, expectantly. Waiting for me to reassure him, yet knowing I was about to break his heart.

"Things feel different. I still love you, but I don't feel in love with you anymore. I think we're better as friends."

This was harder than I thought it would be. I had never been the one to reject someone before, especially someone who I cared for so deeply.

The guilt swept over me like a sandstorm, covering any sign of life with mounds of dust. I had never invested in our relationship fully. I was on a treadmill of self-destruct, sometimes racing ahead, but often running out of steam and feeling like the incline was too high.

Did I even deserve such happiness?

My experience of intimate relationships was a vintage collection of unhealthy boundaries, feeling used and not having any choice. Having someone like James respect me and want to make me feel good was alien to me and I couldn't accept it.

"It's fine. I understand. We'll go back to being friends." His words were articulated like a well-performed script, but you could sense the mourning in the room. Silent grief for the dreams that had been lost.

We hugged, my head pressed deep into his broad chest, his t-shirt soft against my cheek and his aftershave soaking into my pores. I wanted to stay there forever. Lost in the hold of unconditional love. A cruel fate that I should be given the chance to be adored, but too fractured to take it. The character of *best friend* suited me far better.

I sought out others. Someone unavailable to me emotionally, a Peter Pan who was passionate about life, but not about me, younger guys, older guys. It didn't matter. The yoyo between starting relationships with other men, getting hurt, and returning to James for comfort continued for a time to come.

He was a rock for me. A stability and foundation. Yet the draw and excitement of other people still pulled me away.

Maybe this time I would feel whole. Maybe this time I would feel truly worthy. Never quite realising that wholeness and worth came from me not them. The bed of roses that I couldn't quite appreciate because all I saw was my thorns.

Evolution Continues Again

Alongside the back and forth of my tangled love life, being back at school this time was a completely different experience. I was suddenly a mature and interesting older girl. I wasn't the nobody or the dweeb to pick fun of. I was the intriguing one people wanted to get to know.

It was a surreal feeling. I didn't like being the centre of attention, but it made a refreshing break to have people wanting to be friends with me. I was part of something, and I dived in headfirst.

Unfortunately, diving in headfirst can mean cracking your head open on the rocks beneath. I was trying so hard to keep the momentum going, but the stress of coursework was mounting up.

Because of my poor nutrition after the glandular fever and over exercising I had pushed my body into developing chronic fatigue. Even when I was eating better, there was a general malaise and exhaustion that brought brain fog and depression. What was the point of trying to get well? I was fighting a losing battle anyway.

I started restricting my calories again. Caught up in a commotion of feeling out of control and not knowing where I was going, it was the only thing that made sense to me. I was going from one dead-end relationship to another; I couldn't focus on schoolwork and I would return each night to the empty family house. Vacant like my spirit.

I lost weight easily this time. My brain, starved of nourishment and oxygen, couldn't see the reality of how emaciated I was when I looked in the mirror. I still saw that 'bonny' little girl with chunky thighs, no waist. Too much flesh. My body crawled with stinging ants of self-hate and I needed to shrink away. I wanted to peel off my casing to reveal the fruit within. All the while knowing, it didn't matter because I was rotten to the core.

I would pinch my skin in disgust.

Still too fat. Do more sit-ups. Yes, brain, but I'm exhausted. *You're weak and pathetic is what you are! Keep pushing.*

The only barrier to feeling better was the flab that had absorbed all my sins. A barrier of butterfly wing fragility, with breaking point to come.

Mum came around to visit. She was worried about me, as always, but we sat and chatted about school. I showed her some of my coursework I'd done for textiles and protested that I was "doing great."

"Don't stress about me, Mum. I'm fine." My acting impeccable as ever.

"You know you're welcome to come over to our house for dinner any time, don't you?" she encouraged.

I couldn't even remember the last time I'd had dinner.

*

We baked tea bread together. An almost normal act, except this was for her to take home and enjoy. She deserved it more than me.

I went to get another jumper from my bedroom. I was always cold. At the top of the stairs, I'd somehow lost my footing and came tumbling down the mountain of steps like an avalanche. A crumpled heap in the hallway.

Mum rushed out of the front room panic-stricken from the loud thunderous thuds as I'd fallen. She held me like a new-born baby and we both sobbed. "

I don't want to lose another daughter." Like a lightning striking into my soul, snapping my branches and scorching my bark. There it was. The thunderstorm that would charge the electric of my life force. Paddle boards on my lifeless heart, shocking me into action and jolting me from flat lining.

*

My mum had already said goodbye to my sister, a baby that she had birthed after several lost pregnancies and whose heart was too weak to survive. Here I was her second daughter, starving herself and dying slowly in front of her. Another child she wouldn't watch grow. Another child taken too soon. The tragedy was thick like tar in the air. I couldn't put her through it again. Not if I had the choice.

She rocked me in sorrowful lullaby.

"I'm sorry, Mum. I need help." I sobbed.

I had to find a way to rebuild. To start to nourish my body again. To live. To make my mum proud. To honour my sister passed and be what she never had the opportunity to be.

*

We sat there for what felt like hours.

"I'd like to try some of the tea bread I've made, but I'm scared." Food had become my enemy. An army kept out of the castlement of my lips. Calling a truce now and waving a white flag was not going to be easy.

I nibbled the bread in mouse size bites. The flavours and textures hitting my tongue like fireworks. The starchy flour coating my mouth and forcing me into submission. A creamy sheet of surrender injected with moist, soaked sultanas.

It was a ceremony of yielding for us both. Liquid silver tears rolling down our cheeks. As if I was feeding for the first time upon her chest, the relief that something had shifted, and I had latched successfully.

I had taken the first step, but we both knew how defeated I was and how I was going to need more support this time. My mum couldn't be there for me 24/7 and building a skeletal frame back up was not going to be an easy feat.

I was terrified, but I was ready to admit I couldn't do it alone. The embers were burning inside, but they needed more fuel to grow.

The young teenager pierced with experience and illness. The vibrancy of her spring years burned away with the summer but knowing there were shadows cast by the light that needed to be faced. Heading into the season of release, grounding, letting go. Her spirit was to be shaped like the soil, and truths exposed on the surface.

Autumn

Letting go

Life slows and rest follows, melancholy and bittersweet

Dead leaves blanket the floor, protecting roots below with their rugby scrum

The smell of damp decay, must, and smoke fills the air

Harvest, renewal, connection to roots

Chlorophyll wains to expose the golden spectrum beneath

Rainy days with cold wet noses

Wellies kicking crunchy leaves and splashing in puddles

Conkers and pinecones, with helicopters falling

Witches and bats with toffee apple faces

Sparklers, screamers, Catherine Wheels and Guy Fawkes

Warm fires, hot chocolate, syrup porridge and dumpling soups

Darker mornings of grey, with haunting mist on the fields

Letting go, again

Letting Go

We visited the doctor. I was weighed and measured. My BMI was less than 14. My blood pressure barely registered, too shy to beat any stronger.

"I'll put you on the waiting list for the local eating disorder services again. You should hear something in the next few weeks, but it can take up to six months to get an assessment."

Matter of fact 'I've done my job' response.

My chair leg squealed across the lino floor in protest, as I shifted from one sit bone to another. The auburn-haired GP, fresh out of university, sat unaware of the trait that had already kept me alive so long. The sheer bare-faced determination and survival instinct that once present could not be contained, champagne bubbles waiting to explode.

I couldn't wait for six months. In that time my heart would give in because it was already weak and my potassium levels more unpredictable than a ping pong match.

It would be too torturous for me to try re-feeding my body at home alone. I had been trying for days already, and my stomach would become distended like a child with a balloon up their jumper, with cramps stabbing me, hot pokers into my abdomen. My legs would triple in size with oedema and make it unbearable to walk. It wasn't as simple as just "getting a good pan of Scouse down me." I needed to let go of the idea I could do it solo, without anyone's interference.

We had researched available support. I needed somewhere residential that was experienced in helping skeletal figures rebuild. Experts who would be there in those moments of sheer agony and tell me it was going to be ok. Who knew what foods were going to provide nourishment without me having to weigh food, measure or track calories.

The nearest place that had a space was in Aylesbury, 180 miles away. All they needed was a referral from my GP.

My stubborn streak had already decided that this was our solution, and we weren't going to leave that doctor's office until we had the letter sent.

"We can't wait six months because my daughter will be dead by then. We have found somewhere that can take Susie in and help, but we need you to send a referral." You could hear the quake in my mum's voice, holding back the tears. I'd recognised it so much in myself over the years. The sense of fragility that makes your eyes sting and your words weak, but despite her vulnerability, this momma wasn't going to go down without a fight.

"Let me speak with one of our consultants and I'll come back in a moment." Empathy and understanding, the doctor's new foundation colour.

Was someone actually listening to us? Did someone believe in me? She could have told us that they couldn't justify the cost to the NHS, that others needed it more, that I wasn't the only one having to wait, but she saw something in me and drifted out of the room like a falling leaf. Trying her best to land on hopeful grounds.

*

We waited expectantly. Mum taking deep, calming breaths, me internally praying.

The GP's smile entered the room before she did. That was a good sign right? Was it? I'd lost trust in my judgement so opted to wait for her verdict, before getting too excited.

"We can get the referral sent by the end of the day." Her words like party poppers at a surprise celebration. My heart exploding with sheer gratitude alongside.

It wasn't going to be plain sailing, but this was my chance. This was another steppingstone forward and an opportunity to shed the debris that was slowly killing me.

Life Flows and Rest Follows

So here I was, back to where this story began. The Beginning of the End, and Back to the Beginning. But it was far from where my story would end.

The Eating Disorders Centre in Aylesbury. Miles away from everything I ever knew, but closer to becoming myself again.

I arrived full of positivity, enthusiasm and motivation. I was going to follow their programme to the letter, and I would leave there three months later, a different person. I'd already mapped out my vision in my mind.

My room was small and empty, but I didn't see it as a prison cell, as I had done the centre before. I saw it as a cosy den, a sanctuary that was going to be where I would heal. I put photos on the wall, cards from my family and teddies in the bed. Almost homely. A room in a doll's house that you would have to use your imagination to fill with character.

There were three other girls there with me. A compulsive eater, a bulimic and two anorexics. It was normal for us to learn each other's 'conditions' almost before we learned each other's names. It had become our identity. We were victims of dis-ease and it had claimed our names for its own.

I became closest to one of the anorexics, Emma. She was timid and softly spoken with wispy dark hair that framed her face like lace. She spent hours doing embroidery, with minute attention to detail and precision. A fellow perfectionist and creative.

*

It was my first session with the therapeutic team that was going to be the lathe that would shape the following years.

I was ushered into the small office and invited to sit on the royal blue padded chair, a slight rip to its seat, embarrassed to be exposing its cream foam stuffing underneath. No-one else seemed bothered, but I could completely relate to its self-consciousness, as I awaited my initial assessment and planning meeting.

The Centre Manager, a psychologist, and a nutritionist all huddled together, with their notes laid out in front like treasure maps.

I liked the look of the manager, Dr Woods. He reminded me of the BFG. He wasn't tall, in fact was nearly as short as me, but his face was filled with lines of kindness. Highways of happiness and joy. He genuinely cared about the residents at the centre and it showed in his eyes. He had a small grey moustache and a tuft of hair either side of his head like a broken silver crown. He was sat on a black leather office chair. I wondered if he was desperate to spin round on it when everyone left the room, twiddling the edges of his moustache and listening to the top ten on the radio.

The psychologist, Sally, was equally friendly. Her blonde hair in waves around her perfect peach face and her blouse ironed to perfection, with navy blue ruffles around the neck, cheekily rebelling against the straight lines of her pastel blue suit jacket. She perched on the edge of her plastic chair like a cockatoo, legs crossed to steady her, eying up the office chair and possibly wondering the same thoughts as me.

The nutritionist, Mary, was a lady who would take no prisoners. She was from an era of bread and dripping with homemade gravy. Her face crinkled like tin foil and her dark curled hair tight to her scalp, afraid to grow too far away. I hoped she didn't want to make me fat for fun. Lard, on toast every morning.

Thoughts spinning through my mind like tealeaves. Have I done the right thing coming here?

The window was open a notch and a breeze drifted through tickling the rusty curtains and bringing my attention back to the room. Back to my chance of health that I had fought for.

Yes, I've done the right thing.

*

"I'm afraid we're not very hopeful for you." Long, short pause.

"You have already caused excessive damage to your internal organs. Your heart and lungs are weak, and your electrolytes are completely out of balance." Silent, deafening, brief cough.

"Your bones have thinned to that of a seventy-year-old, you have nerve damage to your brain, and you are anaemic. Due to the amenorrhea, you could well remain infertile and never have children." A nettle sting through words. Deep and solemn, but matter of fact.

I remained silent. It wasn't fresh news that I wouldn't be a parent, I had already been told several times by GPs that my lack of periods meant I wouldn't be able to conceive, so the statement left little impact compared to what had already been said. It was the next sentence that was going to be the one I would etch into my brain as a blueprint and a catalyst for change.

"The mortality rate of anorexia is ten times higher than any other cause of death in women before the age of twenty-five." I wasn't quite sure what mortality meant, but it didn't sound good, and Dr Woods, now sullen face, said more to me than his utterings.

"Only one in five sufferers will ever recover, and unfortunately in your current state of health, we don't see you reaching thirty."

Crack! So, it seemed lightning does strike in the same place twice. Another branch descending and a piece of hope conceding with it.

They had little belief in me making it through the next decade?

Give up. No, brain. Not this time *Did you hear what he said? There's no hope for you.*

I was going to prove them wrong. No matter how much suffering I was yet to face, I was not going down without a last crusade.

The bitter reaping of twenty years of seeds being planted in barren soil and growing into the contorted and disfigured shoot that I had become.

Mulch piled high around my roots and insulation around my trunk. Desperate attempts of protection from my mum trying to keep me alive in the world, yet knowing that it was up to me to grow. At some point, I might do this for me, but right now I was doing this for her.

"Then I'll come back and visit you when I've turned thirty." The words sputtered out of me like a leaking pen.

Wow. Defiant, rebellious, fire. Where have you been hidden?

The flames masked underneath the chlorophyll of self-hate, self-doubt and self-annihilation, were starting to show through.

*

I battled daily with thoughts of self-sabotage. I had a stammering voice in my head; you're not thin enough, you need to lose a bit more and everything will be ok. I would pull at my skin, wanting to separate it from my body. Wanting to disappear.

I wasn't ill enough to warrant being here. The other girls had far greater problems than me and I was a charlatan.

I had to find some way of switching off my brain's downward spirals.

I armed myself with distraction techniques like cross-stitch, letters to my family and friends, my diary, self-help books and puzzle books. My concentration levels were extremely low, so I would alternate between manageable activities. The evenings were the hardest and when discomfort would be at its worst.

It will pass, it will pass, it will pass. The bloating will ease off soon, and your body will digest the food and your legs will stop swelling if you elevate them slightly.

Ok. Come on. We can do this.

It was a very slow process, like the last five minutes before you can clock off work, where you can't help but watch the ticking of the minute hand expecting it to go faster. I expected to put on a stone in a week, but only a couple of pounds crept on. How could I eat *that much* food and still only gain a sugar bags worth of weight? This was going to be a long haul and I'd needed to strap myself into the aisle seat and put on an in-flight movie or ten.

*

I was admitted to the nearby hospital several times to try and stabilise my electrolytes and prevent me from cardiac arrest.

My muscles would go weak, nausea take over and my heart become a base drum pounding out of my chest. There was more than one occasion that the doctors gathered around me frantically trying to find veins to insert tubes and get fluids in asap.

At such a low weight my veins were as elusive as a snowy owl and my arms, hands and feet were slowly becoming lost in multi-coloured stains. Tragically beautiful, puffy ink blotches of purple, blue, green, yellow, brown and pink. Rainbows of intervention upon my skin. Another chance. More reinforcement bound around brittle branches.

*

"You're back!" Emma's sunken eyes attempting to light up at the sight of me being wheeled back into the centre on my metal thrown.

"Of course, I'm back. Not ready to check out just yet. I'm gonna take on the world, remember?" Somewhere inside I truly believed that.

I was energised by the fluids plumping out my cells and needed to keep going. One foot in front of the other right? A journey of a thousand miles begins with one step, yes? Well, I'd travelled about half a mile and was already exhausted, wishing I hadn't signed up to this marathon, but reminding myself of the 'runners wall' everyone always spoke of.

You might just do this.

Mentally spitting out my drink all over myself. Sorry brain, can you repeat that?

Even heart was agog.

You might recover. You just need to keep distracting yourself.

Distracting our self from you, you mean? Heart retorted, unable to hold silence any longer.

Awkward cough and squirm. *Erm, yes. From me.*

I'd lost the plot. Hearing voices. Arguing with myself. Wasn't that one of the first signs of madness my mum always spoke of - hearing voices? The second being, answering them back?

I did agree that distraction was a good solution though. Even if only temporary, it took me away from looking in the mirror and hating the fat, skeleton staring back.

It reminded me how I could dissociate away from the agonising surges in my recently reopened, long-disused digestive system, that in reality was a public health and safety hazard.

*

Exercise was limited, so we were only allowed to go for a walk once a week. I loved those walks more than I'd ever loved a walk in my life. Nettie, one of the care workers, would come with me and tell me stories of her life before moving to the UK. She was a wise old oak with a melodic chuckle, and she lifted my spirits on the days when I felt broken.

"I'm so glad to have you here, Nettie."

I really was.

"I believe in you, beautiful girl. Women are warriors. We were not born to suffer as much as we do. You will overcome this, and you will help others do the same." Her angelic smile emanating nurture and comfort.

"I hope so."

I really did.

"There is colour and life even on the wettest and darkest days. We just have to witness it. Take heart in that, won't you?"

I didn't need to respond. Her words cradled me in soft fleecy blankets. A lilt of reassurance. We continued. Silent but held by each other's words.

Stopping to admire violet pansies, huddled together in plant pots like painted meerkats, interspersed with heather like a crowd at a concert.

Transported along cracked pavements by the faint smell of smoke in the air, families gathered around open fires watching movies together. That was me once. That will be me again.

The soothing sound of passing cars on wet roads, rushing past with a serenade of subtle splashes.

We always walked a little bit further than we 'should'. Nettie knew she'd get a slapped wrist, but she wasn't facilitating my demise, she was reminding me about the beauty of life all around me. About stopping to notice the finer details, about opening the senses to a fuller experience, about slowing down and taking your time.

There was magic in those stolen moments. Those windows of space. Those deep inhalations of appreciation.

*

We had sessions with the local chaplain's wife, who would come in and make cards with us as creative therapy. Tables covered with spectrums of ribbons, stickers, scissors and glitter like your favourite craft day at school. Losing yourself in swirls of sparkling silver dust, zigzag cut, handmade paper and sequins glued into position for eye-catching highlights.

I was cautious of her husband for a long while, so ingrained in me the mistrust of men. Little did I know what he would become for me in later years. A mentor and adopted God Dad, who would check in on me daily, and who would love me unconditionally, regardless of what choices I made. His persistence despite being rejected and repelled like a mosquito was admirable, difficult to accept, yet a tonic to my scepticism.

"I want to print out some positive quotes for the walls in the dining room. Can I use your computer please?" I had to let my guard down briefly. He had something I needed, and I wasn't going to get it by continuing to see him as a villain.

"Of course. Nettie can bring you around this afternoon and you can spend an hour or so doing what you want."

The dining room induced such dread in the residents at the centre. It was the place that they would have to do the thing that made their skin crawl with cockroach terror.

The anorexics would have to allow food to pass their lips and swallow it. They would have to sit with that full feeling in their stomach, hating everything that represented to them and wanting to be empty. The bulimics and compulsive eaters would have to eat slowly, and they would have to stop eating at some point, whilst wanting to numb more. It was a torture that you couldn't escape either way.

Some girls hid their golden packeted butter in their napkins or put biscuits down their sleeve when the staff weren't looking, to later dispose of in the bin or down the toilet. Rebellion that was only damaging themselves.

I was an anomaly. I wanted to gain weight at this point. Gaining weight meant going home faster, and I had only come here to get past the re-feeding phase. I welcomed the biggest piece of pie on my plate and the flapjack with the most chocolate chips in. The other girls weren't sure how to take me.

"Aren't you scared of the fat in that? It's got about 500 calories!"

Jane was a frail eighteen-year old who had already been in and out of hospitals since the age of eleven, mostly psychiatric wards that didn't understand eating disorders and would force-feed her like foie gras. She had lost complete trust in the system, and herself. Her dark hair was brittle like spun sugar, her hazel eyes sunken and her cheekbones protruding like a supermodel. The feeling of hopelessness hung over her like cumulonimbus.

"It's just food."

The words came out of my mouth faster than I'd had time to even consider them. Did I even believe them? I wanted to. Maybe I could if I said them enough.

I put the laminated A4 quotes around the baby blue walls.

'You are beautiful', 'You can do this', 'You are powerful', 'You are loved', 'You are brave', 'Everything will be ok'.

I wanted us all to be able to read things to counteract the demons in our head. The voice of doubt. Well-meaning brain, always trying to protect us from perceived threat, but often mistaking what those threats were, like a skittish cat.

The posters stayed on the walls for a long time after I left. I don't know if they helped any of the residents that sat in the feasting room at all.

Maybe the noise of scraping cutlery on plates, the sound of swallowing reluctantly, the feel of the cushioned chairs sucking you in, or the smell of tempting, poison roast dinners overrode any affirmations, but if it helped at least one girl see some hope in it all, I'm proud and glad I did them.

My strength built up very gradually over the first month and by three months I was at a healthy enough weight to consider going home.

I wasn't quite ready, but I missed being in familiar surroundings and my own space, so we formed a plan for me to leave, with continued support local to me. The centre was amazing for lots of things. I gained enough weight for the downy hair on my body to disappear, I had been under observation when re-feeding, that was medically crucial to prevent me having a heart attack, and I'd developed friendships that would last me for years.

Unfortunately, it was also good for introducing me to new patterns of eating that I hadn't previously been aware of.

My body now knew how to binge eat, with strong cravings feeling insatiable at times. I also discovered how to purge. I had never purged before. If I had eaten too much in the past, I only had to cope with the feeling of gluttony. This was a new skill.

I remembered the emetic at the hospital and how cleansed I felt afterwards. Who wouldn't want to feel cleansed sometimes?

A different cycle was to emerge. A new coping mechanism that wasn't always obvious from an outsider's point of view, undetected, secret, mine.

Dead Leaves Blanket the Floor

Returning to the Wirral, I no longer wanted the responsibility of a house on my own. It had been the family home, filled with memories good and bad, but the walls were ready to let go of me. Worn Velcro that no longer stuck. It wasn't the same after my brothers and Mum had left. I thought I could be all grown up and responsible, but really it was another pressure I didn't need to try and handle.

There was so much I wished to be, but I always fell short.

The smell, as I walked through the front door, was toxic and unfamiliar. A combination of fresh paint from the renovation work James had started while I'd been away, new carpets, and citrus fresh release.

It was the same shell I'd always known, but it was different now. Magnolia crisp lines with white radiators as jewellery. The bathroom shiny and pristine, pine perfume, with no dripping tap. The kitchen cupboards with handles gripped tight and youthful. I walked around each room, stroking the cool, smooth walls, pondering what it would be like to stay.

Maybe I could make a go of it here after all? Maybe I had earned a fresh start?

"What do you think?" James stood expectantly waiting for a response.

"It's fab. Almost makes me want to stay!" I laughed, half-jokingly, half-serious.

"You can't. It's already sold to Dave."

Ah yes. Dave. The builder who had looked at it even before the refurb and said he would consider taking it on. He knew it would need the roof fixing and some damp work doing, but it was a steal for him at half the market value. There had been several viewings but no other takers. I could have waited it out, but I had been keen to move on and jumped at the first offer thrown at me quicker than the unwrapping of Christmas presents.

"It's ok. I was only joking. It looks great though, and it's lovely and warm."

I was clearly nesh. Not surprisingly when you have less body fat than a greyhound, but having heating was always on my dream list, and now I was leaving it behind. I remembered so many cold mornings, of virtually sitting on the gas fire, four bars lit, leaving a red glow on my skin until I moved to singe the other leg.

"You've done a good job, James, thank you." Mentally tipping my hat.

"That's what I'm here for." He smiled. Proud and loyal. The doting dog who would sit by your side even if you were lying on the streets. I didn't deserve him in my world.

*

I wanted to try and go back to university and do something productive with my life. I was going to follow the path all my friends had done. To gain respect and direction. I picked subjects that sounded interesting; psychology and sociology. Surely, I couldn't fail at them? I'd got an A in my general studies exam, so I knew it was possible to still achieve something. I just needed to apply myself.

My biggest stumbling block being the thousands sat in my bank from the house sale, ten grand that could have been invested as a deposit for a house in the future, but instead sat there gleaming like forbidden treasure. It turned out to be more of an affliction than good fortune. I could do what I wanted, and it made me reckless with it. I moved into student halls and was out most nights, drinking, binge eating and buying clothes for a wardrobe I never had time to wear.

"Don't worry, Jess, I'll buy dinner and drinks and get us a taxi back. You need to be ready to go at seven." I was *that* cool girl. Suddenly super popular and the one to be around. You'd never go thirsty or bored with me as company. My room mates Jess and Sally loved me.

I would never grow tired of this.

I would fill that weird vacuum I felt inside. All I needed was more things, more people, more food. Torn between being full and being empty. There was comfort in the emptiness; it felt clean and liberating. Weightless, light, clear, but painfully hollow too. Yet I craved the heaviness to numb that periodically, like dirt burying me deep within, protecting me. Dead leaves blanketing my exposed roots.

Mornings spent hungover. Days spent going from one cafe to another. All you can eat buffets of Chinese, chip shops for chips and gravy, sandwich shops for pastry, cookie stands, fast food restaurants for burgers. It didn't matter. They were all good. Never enough in one place for anyone to suspect. I was a regular girl having a large lunch. A healthy appetite. Forbidden foods laced with fat and sugar, processed within an inch of their life. Sedating and soothing.

I was exhausted from another purging session. All energy flushed away with thousands of calories, but I couldn't quite escape into solitary. I emerged from my room to refill my hot water bottle in the kitchen, only to be faced by the bright eyed, bushy tailed Jess.

"We missed you in class today. Mr Greaves gave me this letter to pass to you." A slight tone of delight in her voice, or was that me imagining things?

Thanks, Jess. As if I needed a reminder that I was there to work. I binned the letter. I'd face it tomorrow, I decided.

There were many tomorrows.

I was a failure who was just too different to ever fit in. Realistically university wasn't what I wanted, or what was going to help me progress. I went to classes, but my mind was constantly elsewhere, planning my next binge. Passing the time away mindlessly. Something had to give.

Damp Decay Fills the Air

I was still going out most weeks and moving from one casual relationship to another.

I became a chameleon, fitting into whatever was expected of me, for the sake of perceived love in return. It didn't matter, because whatever I faced, I could purge it out at some point with food.

I finally gave up the burden of uni and moved in with my brother. It was fine. I didn't want to be the same as everyone else anyway. It wasn't as if a degree got you anywhere in life these days. I knew several people who'd ended up working in minimum wage jobs once they'd graduated. I had better things to do.

*

I met a guy online from Northampton and travelled to stay with him several times over a few months, maybe this was the one? Ben Chapman. Dark hair, dark eyes, bright smile. Everyone's best friend. The joker and the lad. I'd met him on 'Hot or Not' and he'd thought I was 'hot'. That was enough for me.

Susanne Chapman. That sounded pretty cool. I'd have to start practising my new signature. I predicted good things this time. This was my part as *long-distance lover.*

Ben was as charming as a pungi. I was yet to discover he was the python hypnotising me though. I completely trusted him and gave him what was left of the money from the sale of the house to buy me a ticket to travel with him to Australia, so caught up in the romance and wistful dream.

Then he wasn't answering my calls or texts.

I was sleeping at his friend's house in the empty bed we'd shared.

"Have you heard from Ben?" I asked.

A scruffy Jake, with eyes peeping through his dreadlocked hair, carrying a chipped mug of coffee and half-smoked roll-up was caught slightly off guard. His eyes were still fighting the daylight and pulling the blinds shut.

"Err, no, sorry." He genuinely did look sorry. A well-practised look that didn't seem unique to be being acted out.

"It's not your fault. It's just he went to get my tickets for Oz, and I need to go home and get my passport sorted."

"Oh." That did not sound a good oh. Was there such a thing as a good oh? I don't know, but this certainly wasn't one of them. It was a flat note in a beautiful concerto, a bitter strawberry in a bowl of sweetness, a jagged rock underfoot on a smooth calm beach.

"Oh?" A question I wasn't sure I wanted to ask.

"How much did you give him exactly?"

"Two grand."

I didn't think Jake could get any paler than his usual anaemic and ghostly shade, but somehow even the whitest tones drained from his face and his freckles vanished with them, abandoning their post, absent without leave.

"I don't think you'll see him again, sorry."

What? He was kidding, right? How could someone disappear without a trace? With the money that was for a dream adventure, from the girl who was the angel in his world?

My legs capsized beneath me, a sinking ship with no lifeboats and no life jackets. Jake went on to explain to me about Ben's cocaine addiction, how he would go off the rails periodically, and they wouldn't hear from him for months. I was one bead in a string of unsuspecting orbs.

The last bit of the monetary legacy of my childhood gone, just like that. A dream of seeing more of the world crushed into naive powder and arrogantly snorted. I could hear the laughter through my gullible and desperate veneer. How was I ever going to trust again?

The long-distance lover would be abandoned and left to go home alone once more. No more train journeys of anticipation and excitement would follow.

*

Some guys did love me, but I struggled to accept that now. Somehow, I felt more at ease with questioning myself constantly, the paranoia, the fear of rejection, the jealousy. It gave me reason to stay locked in my destructive patterns. It made more sense to me. Life was cruel, but I needed to get on with it. Those that were nice, would get rejected and hurt. Those that were abusive became my drug of choice.

Internally battling with a dialogue of wanting to change things, of knowing that the self-destruction had to stop.

That having someone love you, despite feeling completely unworthy, was ok. That being screamed at or strangled when trying to leave, was not ok.

It was a cycle of doing better, being in control more and getting support through counselling, then ending up sucked back into the eating disorder and accepting narcissism and abuse as the norm.

At some point, I had to take off the mask of green and allow the true colours underneath to shine through. I needed to let some things go. The leaves were trying to fall, but I clung on for dear life, a bulldog with a bone.

The ground was holding me, my roots beneath the earth. I was safe. I needed to start branching out.

What did I want to do with my life? Did I want to stay in admin and spend the next sixty years working 9 to 5 and having two weeks holiday a year?

My frivolity had to stop. The money had run out. I hadn't bought any lasting friendships or cleansed away any of the self-hate, regardless of how many times I had flushed the chain to wash away my purge.

*

I received news that one of the girls I had been in the eating disorder centre with had passed away, Kate. It was Kate who taught me about purging. She was a beautiful and broken soul. Abused by family members growing up and unable to see such little worth left within herself as a result. We understood each other and the thought of her losing the battle was a knife to the chest.

She had stopped purging, drinking and taking drugs, she had got her own flat and a job. She was doing well, but the damage had already been done. Her body was defeated, and her heart gave out, despite her recovery. It was a huge wake-up call. Another one. I was a cat with nine lives, but I was running out of lives fast. I couldn't outrun death every time and I knew it.

Harvest

I looked back on what I had already done, and where I felt truly happy. I remembered how I received Reiki when I first had glandular fever and been housebound with ME. It was the first time in as long as I could remember that I had felt calm and at peace.

I wanted to offer people the same sanctuary. I found a tutor and signed up for her next course. This was something for me. There was no pressure or expectations and I came out of the training feeling euphoric. I felt so present, clarified and content without the need for starvation to produce that.

*

I volunteered at a local cancer services centre offering treatment and felt pride in what I was doing. Seeing patients suffer, without choice, brought home to me how precious life was, and how you need to grab every opportunity with both hands. I had wasted so much time already. How selfish I had been.

My manager, Carol, was a lovely lady. Softly spoken, gentle and warm. Her whole essence oozed ocean wave tranquillity. The centre was a home away from home for many, with plush silver cushions upon plum comfy couches, subtle lighting in amber tones and framed pictures of woodland scenes and sunsets. Even her office was a beautiful haven of sky-blue walls, maple furniture and cream ornamental accents. The cerise flowers upon her desk composed and serene.

"I just wanted to say what a wonderful job you're doing here, and how many people you are helping with your time."

My heart glowed.

"I'm not sure if you have considered it, but if you offered even more therapies, then I know you would never be out of work. All of our clients have nothing but good things to say about you, and you have such a calm demeanour about you, that they feel instantly relaxed in your sessions."

I might have cried if my tear ducts had let me.

"That's the nicest thing anyone has said to me for a long time. Thank you, Carol."

I went home and researched courses for massage and reflexology. Carol believed in me and I had to start believing in myself. I had spent months trying to help increase the quality of life for those enduring chemotherapy, so I needed to start reaping some of that quality of life back for myself.

A new path had been laid out in front of me. The streetlights had been switched on and I needed to change my course of direction. This was a huge incentive for me to focus on *my* health more.

You can't help others until you help yourself. Yes brain, wise words. Let's do this.

I found some massage courses at a college in Manchester. It was intensive training so I would be fully qualified within a year if I studied hard enough and applied myself. A year was nothing compared to how much time I'd already spent attempting university and trying to follow the traditional route of education.

Maybe this could be a fresh start for me? Manchester wasn't far and the accommodation was cheap enough there. I might as well gather my crops of momentum and go for it.

*

It was a new challenge, filled with possibility and potential. I got a job managing the school and therapy centre that I was studying in and started to feel valued and appreciated.

The manager was an intriguing man, a slight frame, with a morose tone, jet black shoe polish hair and dark eyes scrunched up like candy wrappers. He spent most of his time locked away in his room, monitoring everything on his collection of CCTV cameras like National Intelligence. He would come out to bark orders at us occasionally, but we were generally left to it.

It was a great group of girls working there. We all had our stories to share; we all supported each other learning the therapies and gaining experience, and we all had a good giggle together.

"It's your turn to clean the bathrooms for two rupees an hour today!" Gail gave a cheeky smile and flicked her silver blonde hair out of her eyes.

We divided the jobs between us, and all did our bit, but watching her and Donna procrastinate and tease each other was priceless.

"Aww, man. Can't I change the treatment table covers or empty the bins? The toilets are grim! I'm sure I saw a hair monster crawling about waving a white flag in there last week!"

"You might find some bonus toenails in the room corners or snot stains on the walls. You could make a collage out of them all to put up in the hallway. Call it 'The Last Supper'."

"Gross, Gail. Just gross!"

Donna pretended to heave at the thought, then we all burst out laughing, and carried on sharing our box of thank you fudge brought in by one of the clients. Definitely not toenail flavoured.

I'd never been part of a group of women so supportive of each other. Even the horrible jobs were easier with a sense of humour and a sisterhood. It was something I'd craved for a long time, without even realising, but I'd stopped dreaming was possible.

Someday I would recreate that sense of sisterhood on a larger scale and help others feel part of something. It was liberating. It didn't matter how much our boss moaned at us, or how rude clients were, we held each other together and were always reminded how to laugh and smile.

*

I was still binging and purging, but less frequently. It was a habit ingrained into my weekly life that I wasn't ready to let go of yet. Control, control, control.

I was somehow managing to hold things together regardless. I worked hard. I managed a team. I was needed. I couldn't give in to total self-destruct, but it still lingered like stale garlic in the air. Not ready to be stored for winter yet.

Connection to Roots

My partner at the time, Joe, was insecure. He had been another exciting prospect. It was attractive to start with, that he was so needy of my attention and wanted to spend every moment he could with me. This was my chance to play *rescuer*, not knowing that in time it would become stifling.

I had made friends both in work and online and he couldn't cope. His behaviour became more and more chaotic.

I would come home and find he had cut chunks of his hair off, saying that he knew I preferred short hair.

We would go on nights out with his friends and he would take ecstasy and drink until he would pass out and have a fit. It was left to me to sit with him in the accident and emergency department with nurses frowning and tutting at me, muttering how much time they wasted helping reckless teenagers on drugs. It was also left to me to explain to his parents what on earth had gone on.

"His drink was spiked"

"He hadn't had dinner before we left, so the alcohol went to his head quicker."

"He was just doing a drinking dare."

Justifications for behaviour that resulted from him wanting to numb his anxieties. I understood. I stayed for months watching him torture himself, hoping I could reassure him enough to change, but I was exhausted and depleted.

*

"I'm leaving. I can't do this anymore. We're not good for each other."

His face contorted into a wail and a dark cloud descended around us both. He pulled out a shard of glass from his pocket and started to pierce his arms with rejection and self-hate.

"You can't go. I'm nothing without you. I know you fancy Craig more than me. Is that where you're going? I'll come to find you. You can't leave. He can't have you. Nobody else can. They wouldn't put up with you anyway. You're nothing without me." His words attacking me like typist's hands on a keyboard. Was he even stopping for air?

Drips of crimson fell upon the beige carpet. I wasn't going to get my deposit back. I should have felt remorse. I should have felt concern. I should have rushed to him, and held him, and nursed his wounds, but all I could do was stand there, stunned. A frozen statue desensitized to trauma.

"Please stop. You don't need to do this. You will be ok. I'll ring your parents. They can come and get you."

He fell to the floor and curled into a ball, crying as if he was letting out generations of sadness.

"I'm so stupid. I should have known. Stupid, stupid, stupid." He was hitting himself in the head and rocking backwards and forwards.

I wanted to go to him. I wanted to take away his pain. I was being callous and brutal by merely observing, but something inside me knew that if I did try to soothe his insecurity, I would be there ten years later doing the same.

I didn't know how serious he was about taking his life. I had done the whole self-harm thing so many times, wanting someone to witness how much pain I felt inside. I hoped this was just him trying to express the same, but I didn't want to be responsible for dealing with a more serious outcome.

*

The phone rang for eleven long rings. Answer the phone.

Come on. Answer the phone. "Hello?" A calm question. A mother unaware of her son's current state of mind. An illusion of life's order about to be shattered.

"You need to come and get Joe. He's not in a good way. I can't help him and I'm going tonight." My voice shaking with assertion.

"Can I speak to him?" Still calm. Had she been here before? Was this a normal part of life's order for them? "We'll come and collect him tomorrow morning if you can just hide anything sharp and stay with him for the night please?" Hide anything sharp? It was too late for that. She had been here before. I handed the phone to Joe, hearing her voice pierce his chaos.

"It's your mum, Joe. It's ok."

It wasn't ok. Nothing about this situation was ok, but that's one of those phrases that come out of your mouth unexpectedly when you don't know what else to say. The 'I'm fine', 'you look great', 'I'm just tired' type phrases.

I left them to talk. Just faintly hearing "I'm sorry, Mum. I'm so sorry."

This was as much my fault as his. I didn't reassure him enough. I didn't give him enough attention. I spent too much time chatting with friends in the evenings when I should have been chatting with him. I was a lousy girlfriend and a useless rescuer.

I packed a couple of bags and stuffed them in the wardrobe. An inmate awaiting jailbreak.

Joe had said on more than one occasion that he couldn't bear the thought of me with anyone else. He swore he'd never hurt me, but his behaviour was so turbulent that all I could think about was him trying to take my life as well as his own. He knew I wanted to go, so what did he have to keep me alive for?

This would require some acting skills now. He couldn't catch on to my plan. His parents would arrive the next morning, but that could be too late for me. The newspapers splashed with headlines about the tragedy of it all. I had gone through the kitchen and bagged up all the knives, I had taken the razors from the bathroom, and I had put our medicine cabinet into the black sack with them. Thankful that our rubbish was concealed from the world and dumped in the bin outside. My fear bundled up in a balloon of ammunition.

*

I walked back into the front room. Joe was cat-curled on the couch. His arms now crusted with blood but no longer seeping. His tears stopped, but droplets still attempting to fall from his nose, only to be sniffled back up for safekeeping.

"I'm ok now. My mum and dad are coming tomorrow, and I'll be out of your life for good." His eyes glazed over staring at the floor.

How could I be so cruel? I sat next to him and stroked his head. He would be ok. He would be better with me out of his life for good. I carried storm clouds with me that brought destruction and pain to others. I was better alone. Then I couldn't hurt anyone else.

He drifted off and after a while, I joined him.

My twisted neck waking me at 3 am with stabbing pain and reminding me of my escape plan. It didn't seem as urgent now, but I didn't want to face his parents again either. With ninja stealth I extracted myself from the sofa and gathered up my things, shoving them into my boot and clicking it shut with hushed gestures. A silencer on the weapon terminating another chapter.

My banana yellow Seicento rattled along the motorway. My faithful ally and accomplice. I needed to get back to the Wirral. Back to my roots. Back to some sense of security and familiarity.

It was the middle of a blizzard; the snow was horizontal like the ending credits of Buck Rogers, hypnotic and mesmerising. I was exhausted and terrified I would crash but had to keep driving. I opened my windows and kept praying that, somehow, I would make it back to my mum's flat alive.

How had I got myself into a situation like this? How could I be so stupid again? I was doomed to end up running away constantly. One broken relationship to another.

*

Somehow, I did make it. I had a key to the flat and let myself in at 4.15 am. Not a sound in the building except for the grinding of cables as my lift crept up and the humming of the broken light in the corridor. I had packed my bags on my back like a camel and shuffled to the door like a navy seal in training. This was the last test and I'd passed.

I collapsed onto the bed, spent and bruised. I would sleep solidly now for nine hours. Dreaming away the nightmare of the last twenty-four.

I never had contact with Joe after that night, but his mum rang to let me know that he was getting help and to thank me for being there for him. I didn't feel like I'd been there for him. I felt that I'd just caused him more problems, but I told her she was welcome regardless.

Friends rallied round to get the last of my things and hand my keys back to the landlord. There was no sign of Joes belongings and the door was closed. Sealed shut as if it never happened. A tomb of regret, but also realisation.

I couldn't save anyone but myself.

Rainy Days and Crunchy Leaves

My dad was getting married for the third time. To Liz. We hadn't spoken much recently, but I was still invited to the party afterwards.

Unfortunately, it came at the same time that my smear results did. Diagnosis: 'dyskaryosis', changed cells, pre-cancerous, but in need of loop excision to remove them. I had received regular smears since the news of my sexual relationships from the age of thirteen had come out in counselling sessions. There was already damage to the cervix, and this had confirmed that it was causing further issues.

*

Sitting in the murky beige room, on chairs designed to shape you into a crooked branch, with posters dotted around, bold letters of CANCER written on each one. Threatening the inevitability of your death sentence as you sat there waiting for your name to be called.

Heat poured out of the air conditioning vents groaning a dull tone, and blue bodies rushed around clicking pens, with important things to do. There was something about waiting rooms that always brought me out in a cold sweat. Waiting for the hand of fate to decide what was next.

"Just to make you aware, there will be slight discomfort and bleeding after the operation. The ache will be like period pains and should ease after five days or so."

I simply nodded. It was that or more advanced therapy later down the line, so my choices were limited.

The procedure was over in ten minutes and I was sent home with an advice leaflet, making room for the next lady to be treated.

There was a slight underestimation on the discomfort scale, and very little discussion about the black clots I would have pouring from my body, burnt blood that felt endless, the tainted remains of my experience as a fresh teenager. Somehow an appropriate afterthought.

*

"Are you nearly ready yet?" James was driving us to the party, so understandably wanting to leave handy, to ensure we got a decent parking space.

He was still my knight in shining armour, and he continued to wear his suit well.

“I’ll be out in a minute!” I was dressed, but doubled over in the bathroom, more ten-tonne weights being dropped on my womb from a great height, crushing me underneath.

“Do you want any more paracetamol?” James called. I’d already taken six and was constantly aware of causing damage to my liver.

“No, I’m fine. The pain is easing now.” That was a lie, but at least he wouldn’t feel so helpless.

The venue was set up with tables adorned with silver balloons bobbing in sync to the music, wedding confetti and red glitter scattered across their white table-clothed tops. The room was filled with faces, most of whom I couldn’t recognise, all beaming smiles.

“You made it!” Liz pulled me in for a rather sloppy kiss and squeezed the last bit of breath from my lungs. Always enthusiastic and keen, always well-meaning.

“You look beautiful, Liz.” She really did. She was glowing. A radiance of happiness that I could see my dad had caught too.

I hugged him as well. Not quite as eager on his behalf. The kind of hug you get from someone who sees it as an unnecessary interaction, foreign to them and awkward.

I was glad that he’d found someone who valued him and truly loved him. Even with the animosity we’d shared, I still wanted him to settle down and experience some positivity.

“I can’t stay long sorry, Dad.”

The pad I had used was already soaked through with blood, and I hadn’t had the foresight to put any more in my bag. The pains were overwhelming me and making me dizzy and nauseous. I needed my bed and a hot water bottle.

The despondency crept across his face. He didn’t understand why having a ‘minor operation’ would stop me from celebrating with the family.

The resentment between us both, hung there, a rotting apple on a tree of bitterness. He would always want more from me. I would always want more from him. I was sensitive. He was pragmatic.

I hated him at that moment. I should have been delighted for him, but all his many words of wisdom strobed through my mind.

‘Don’t worry about what people think of you.’ ‘You just need a good pan of stew to sort you out.’ ‘Your family should be your priority.’ Reminders of how different we were.

Raindrops falling on sunny days to prompt you not to be complacent. The crunch underfoot reflecting the crunch of your heart in times of being misunderstood.

He never forgave me for not going to my grandad's funeral. I never forgave him for not being there for me as a child. Now he wouldn't forgive me for leaving his wedding early, and I wouldn't forgive him for not understanding the agony I was in. I walked away.

Blood pouring down my legs like inconsolable tears. I no longer needed his approval.

Darker Mornings

I was still working in Manchester but now living at my mum's flat in Moreton. I didn't mind the commute. It was thinking time.

Some days I would binge eat en route then purge when I got to work, empty for the day until I got home and binged again. It didn't matter what I binged on. I'd bake cakes, make a whole tray of bread with oil and beans, have huge pans of pasta with vegetables, bags of broken biscuits, fruit, cereal. Anything to fill the void temporarily. Some days the cycle didn't drag me in, and I would get through 72 hours without being sick.

I was still feeling lost, looking for security and stability, and I met a guy who promised to give me both. It was slightly different than any relationship I'd been in before. We met as friends and I spilled out my whole life to him in a waterfall. I couldn't play any more games or be with someone hiding elements of my life. He knew about the sexual abuse, the physical violence of other relationships, the eating disorder, my broken relationship with my dad. Every dark secret I'd held onto for two decades poured out of me.

It didn't faze him at all. There was a magic between us and a spark that resonated throughout the room when we were together. He accepted me exactly as I was.

"I want to help you. I know that I can. Just trust me." I did trust him, and I would be his *subservient.* Simon was slight in build, with long dark hair and deep mahogany eyes that you could get lost in for days. He reminded me of an ancient warrior. Mysterious and strong, yet gentle and reassuring. He helped me begin to shift away from the destruction I put my body through by giving me hope that things could be different. There was power in that hope. It was something I had long forgotten about.

I loved Simon like I'd never loved anyone. He was intoxicating. He was my drug of choice and I didn't care what comedown I would have to face.

"I love you, hubby."

"I love you, wifey."

Of course, we weren't married, but we were dedicated to each other completely and immersed in each other for a long time. Blinded by the chemistry, the connection, the unconditional acceptance.

He would distract me with conversation on the days when I wanted to purge, tell me how beautiful I was on the days I felt fat, reassure me when I was masked in self-doubt. I really believed he loved me, and we felt invincible together. We didn't notice the paranoia set in, the insecurity, the co-dependence, the anger, the resentment.

He got frustrated if he hadn't had weed for a few days, and he was grumpy when he'd had a drink, but I was oblivious to how that would snowball into darker times moving forward.

A lot of it is a blur. A lot of it has been blocked out. A lot of it was brushed off as my imagination, gaslighted and twisted into an exaggerated story. I would leave him several times, then go back, still addicted to the high, despite the lows that followed. Some friends begged me to leave. We weren't good for each other. We were no longer intoxicating, just toxic.

"I can't leave him. I love him."

"This isn't love. This is desperation. It's a sickness."

"You don't understand the connection we have. I've never experienced that type of bond before. How could I walk away from that? No-one else understands me the way he does. I'm broken goods, who else would take me?"

There was no rationalising with me. This wasn't a rational situation or one with a straightforward answer.

The fights got more intense; the games started, the fear started, the punishments bigger. The passion was all-consuming, but so was being pinned against the wall by my throat, being locked in his flat or gaslighted to believe I was going crazy. I was reminded of how painful love was. Rarely overtly. I never carried many bruises on my skin. I reached the depths of self-doubt. Buried deep in the dirt of my soul. Unsure how to dig my way back out.

The mornings were dark, and they bled far into the night. Stars trying to shine through in the black but obscured by clouds of anger and hate. Where was my torchlight to find my way out now? Where was the moon smiling his sweet face in the twilight? I was lost in the cavern, no idea where to turn.

I had been prepared to be accommodating without question in order to feel loved. Yet here I was, a hollow tree, clinging on to dead wood.

Letting Go Again

I had to emerge from the cocoon that had formed around me. Fireworks were going off in my soul. Bursting to get out. I had to let this go. The dead wood was slowly killing me with it.

It was time to be stripped bare and learn to stand strong in my own trunk, with my own root systems that didn't cling to another's. I had some work to do.

I had no idea what tree I even was anymore. I had tried on so many characteristics, become so entwined in others branches and starved of nutrients that I wasn't sure what my own natural form was.

Some would take that as a reason to be sprayed with a blue cross and chopped down, but this was my chance to decide what I wanted to be. Evergreen and bold or deciduous and soft, a tree for others to climb upon or a shelter from the hot sun, a tree to bear fruit or one to blossom. Maybe I could be a combination of it all.

The young woman ashamed by her actions, her structure, broken and reshaped. Letting go of victimhood, self-destruction and abuse and entering the season of stillness. Her summer years long gone but scorch marks remaining, her autumn years waning away with just a few leaves of self-doubt clinging on to the branches.

Winter was coming and her spirit was to be released, communicated to the world, breath by breath. Her trunk needed to be strong to face the storms ahead and her roots deep in the ground to envelop the seedlings beneath. There would be no more hiding behind excuses. This was the time to build a legacy and grow in wisdom and strength.

Winter

Standing tall

Growth inhibited by environmental stress, a time of reflection in icy waters

Seeds stay dormant in a state of deep rest

Roots anchored deep in the earth, wise and frozen in time

The decline of darkness begins, and hope presents itself in glistening tree lights

Mandalas of frost displayed on windscreens, proud of their beauty

Family, comfort, traditions and celebration

Trees bare and exposed, yet strong and immortal

Bobble hats, mittens, rosy cheeks and snuffles

With the smell of mince pies, fudge and mixed spice as a side note

Emerald green with blood red holly

Pantomimes, grottos, wrapping paper mountains

Auld Lang sein, fireworks and promising resolutions

Standing tall, again.

Standing Tall

I moved back to my brother's again. A solid base to rebuild from. The winds were shifting, blowing away the last of the decaying leaves and bringing in the crisp new reality of days unfolding.

Things were about to change in so many ways. It would be the last year I would go on holiday with James and things were going to be very different now.

He had met a girl called Sophie on one of our holidays to Egypt and she had been messaging him since she got home. Suddenly he wasn't just my best friend, with no distractions. He was a desirable man whose attention was being drawn elsewhere.

We went on a holiday to Malta with my mum and stepdad, but for the first time, he was tied to the expectations of someone else. He was asked to phone her every evening to check-in and spent a lot of his time doing this. A movement in reality had happened, and I needed to accept it.

I couldn't rely on him to always be there to pick up the pieces anymore. It was a bitter pill to swallow and I wasn't quite ready to concede yet.

"I miss you." I pined.

"I'm still here." James hugged me, but his embrace was softer now, his arms didn't quite wrap around as much, the ivy bind between us dying.

"You don't need me now. You have Sophie."

I had no right to be jealous. I had rejected him countless times. He was finally happy. Why couldn't I be happy for him? Because I wanted to be happy like that. Not fractured, damaged goods.

"I'll always be here for you." He said it with such confidence and certainty, that it melted a thousand fears.

Do you really believe that? Oh brain, can you give it a break?

We need to believe it. Thank you, heart. We do.

*

I wasn't supposed to make it this far. I had been told I wouldn't make it to thirty and yet here I was nearing the end of my third decade.

I didn't return to the centre in Aylesbury, but I did write them a letter to say thank you for giving me such determination to fight for my life.

I had to celebrate.

With the belief that any year from this day forward would be classed as a bonus, I decided to write a bucket list.

It would include all the things I had been scared to do, put off or believed were out of my remit.

*

Number One - Ride a horse.

I was terrified of how big and powerful they were. The bold dark eyes staring you down and sizing you up to see if they thought you were fair game. The sheer size of them domineering the airspace, with the ability to flick you off the planet like a flea at any moment. I booked a lesson.

"This is your horse for today's session. Her name is Midnight."

Obvious really. She was a huge pure black mare, eyelashes to die for, and a mane plaited into twisted perfection.

"Can I stroke her?"

What a stupid question. I was about to sit on her back and tap my heels into her ribs, and I'm wondering if I can stroke her.

"Of course."

Of course. Lisa smiled a friendly smile. A little wonky, probably due to my pea-brained request, but beautiful despite the metal braces framing her pearly whites. She was very much a horse person. No makeup needed, pale brown thick leggings and olive green, fur-lined gilet over her grey jumper. I wished I had her confidence. She didn't need to look like a model on a magazine cover. She was naturally pretty and comfortable in her skin regardless.

"Midnight has a lovely temperament, and I'll talk you through everything don't worry."

Maybe I could do this after all.

Lisa went on to explain how to mount a horse correctly, my riding position, and how to clutch the reins properly.

Who knew it was this complicated? Whenever I'd seen it on TV, they had made it look effortless.

She led me on a gentle walk around the yard to help me get a feel for the movement. My hands gripped tight until my knuckles were white, and my jaw ached from the tension, but I got through thirty minutes without passing out or being thrown off, so that was my first win.

Number Two - Learn to dance.

I had to prove the ballet teacher wrong. Music ran through my bones like static electricity whenever I heard it. I had to move. A reflex response to the beat and the melody, jolting my hips to spasm and twitch.

My friend Joanne encouraged me to try modern jive.

"I go every week. It's great fun. You should come!" Her enthusiasm resembled that of the staff in the Disney Store.

"Modern Jive? Isn't that for old people?" I imagined a room full of elderly bingo players, performing kicks and flicks with pins curls and bryl cream.

Joanne laughed. "No! It's all ages. They play the latest music and it's easy to learn. Come try it once and if you don't like it you don't have to come again."

"Ok. Deal. What do I wear?"

"Anything you feel comfortable in."

Well, that would be fun. I didn't feel comfortable in anything. Black leggings and sparkly top it was.

We walked into the hall and my heart pounded. I was really here. I was going to join a line of complete strangers and try to learn a dance that I'd never even studied on YouTube. Maybe I could just say I needed the toilet and make a swift escape.

*

"Lovely to see a new face. What's your name?" The lady on the door was radiant with welcoming ease. Her eyes glistening under the flashing lights around the room, lightening my anxiety. Maybe I could stay for the lesson.

"Erm, S-Susanne," I stammered.

"We'll look after you here, don't worry. We're a friendly bunch, and we love newcomers." Thank goodness for that.

Joanne had special dance shoes in a little black bag. I wondered if I'd ever have a little black bag like that. It somehow felt like a sign that you were a serious dancer. A trophy symbol that you'd made it. That was my new goal.

There was a full spectrum of people of all ages, more women than men, but that suited me fine and felt less predatory. The music was familiar with lots of current tracks and the steel girders in my body started to melt a bit, releasing the rigidity of my frame.

We ran through four dance moves that would be repeated over and over within a dance.

"Any mistakes are the guy's fault, remember ladies. It's up to them to lead you correctly."

I liked that idea. I was off the hook if I stood on their toes or fell in a heap on the floor. It was ok to make mistakes.

By week three, I was addicted, and I started going alone. I didn't need to learn any fancy footwork; I could let the man lead me and dance. That freedom was liberating. A fallen leaf gliding across the floor, letting the wind hold me and guide me.

*

Number Three - Go travelling alone.

I may have lost the money saved for Australia, but I was still desperate to see what I could of the world, and I knew I had to push myself to do it alone. I spent days on the internet doing research and deliberating where I was going to go first. My uncle was in Norway so I could visit him, but the food would be a problem there. Maybe Paris again, because I'd only had a two-day trip with James there last time and it was amazingly magical, but the language barrier would make me anxious. Final option then, Ireland.

I found bus tours that included hostel accommodation, you could cook your own meals, and there were no language issues to evade me. It was still a plane flight away, and the first time I was to fly alone, so it felt a good fit. All I needed to do was to pack a rucksack for a five-day trip. I was to be a cool backpacker, braving the world like an explorer. Who would have thought it?

Sat on the plane I felt a rush of achievement. I'd done it. I was doing it. Alone. I had watched movies of women going on wild adventures alone, a retreat for the soul, but I never thought I would be sat there doing it myself.

*

I arrived in Dublin with its shiny cobbled streets, overflowing pubs and narrow bridges, the atmosphere lively and exciting. Laughter and music blared out of windows, buskers sang lilting songs near shop doorways, and crowds of Japanese tourists snapped photos of every Irish detail they could find.

I negotiated my way to the hostel on the email I'd printed out. Dark green doors, one side open and the other still asleep. A huge grey building with ornate decorations carved in the stone around the window frame. It reminded me of Liverpool.

"Top of the morning to ya!"

Did they really say that? Well, apparently so, according to the small auburn-haired pixie man on the front desk at least. Dimples like potholes in his cheeks and laughter lines running parallel on his cheekbones. He wore a jumper that looked very scratchy, but it somehow felt rude to ask him if it was.

"My names Jimmy. Can I take your booking?"

I handed him my folded confirmation and waited while he tapped away on his computer. I could smell bacon and eggs simmering as an afterthought. Someone was playing the guitar somewhere near, and there were tapping footsteps as accompaniment. It was a far cry from the hostel I'd stayed in when rained off from a festival in Scotland. I distinctly recalled putting my keys and money in my sock when I'd stayed there. This was more of a hip hotel for trendy travellers.

I could start to feel my backpack digging into the pads of my shoulders. I may well have packed a few too many hoodies.

"You're in room 20. I'll show you the way."

I followed scratchy jumpered Jimmy up the stairs. Random people sat on the steps on the first-floor writing song lyrics together. We edged past them and Jimmy opened the door to room 20.

My initial thought when I saw the collection of bunk beds was a mixture of prison and school camp. I was to find an empty bed and claim it as my own by simply putting some of my stuff on it. I went near to the window. I needed to know I had an escape route if necessary. Brain always looking at keeping me safe.

I perched on the edge of the wafer-thin mattress. The room was empty. Thoughts of sheer panic started to creep in, and I wondered why I ever thought this would be a good idea. What would I do now? I was in a different country, oblivious to where I was, and I didn't have a clue how I was going to get through another five minutes, let alone five days.

Time went in slow motion. I'm pretty sure at one point it even skipped back a few minutes just to torture me.

My stomach churned into butter, I desperately text friends from home, pretending it was all so amazing, while inside hoping they would say how much they missed me, and give me a reason to go home. The only reply coming through from my mum, saying to have a great time, while everyone else was either in work or still asleep.

*

When I thought I might spontaneously implode with anxiety, a group of American girls and an Austrian guy came into the room.

Full of energy and infectiously happy. The cloud that sat over me lifted within minutes as they cooed over my 'funny accent' and asked a dozen questions about where I was from and what I did for a living.

It took me back to the first day of school when I returned to do my A-levels. Being different wasn't always a smear on your character, sometimes it was a novelty, and I was their interesting specimen to examine.

They had landed in Ireland after a tour of England and loved how 'quaint' everything was. They were to take me under their wing, like seasoned pros of the whole backpacking tour scene, and show me how to party each night.

*

The first night in Dublin was probably one of the most fun nights out I'd ever had. I didn't have anything to prove to anyone; no-one knew me, and no-one knew my history. I decided not to drink because I didn't want to run the risk of feeling sick while away, but I didn't need to drink to have fun, and I could dance the night away with some fellow adventurers.

We would travel by coach from one part of Ireland to another, collecting new friends along the way. All with the same happy go lucky attitude and welcoming nature. Everyone was here for the same reason. Some alone, some with groups. There was no need for animosity or judgements, because wherever we went and whoever we met, it was all temporary and you would probably never see them again.

*

I became close with an Australian guy, Tom, who loved to take photos. He was bubbly, funny, and full of energy. Everywhere I turned he'd be there with his camera and it was inspirational to have someone that loved to capture life's moments as much as I did.

He had done a lot of travelling and would be doing the Europe tour next. He encouraged me to book the tour too.

"We can meet up while you're there, ay?"

"Yeah sure, why not?"

I was half-joking, half-serious. Maybe I would get away from the grip of Simon after all. Tom was an excited puppy and I couldn't resist the charm of it all.

I would have to return home and back to the reality of my life eventually, but in Ireland I was free. There was a beauty that lay in those green hills and craggy cliffs that I haven't experienced since. For a country that has lived through such hardships such as famine and hostility, they create such happy Irish jigs and are so welcoming and hospitable as a culture. It felt familiar. Like my own roots, like my own life.

Battered and weathered by storms, yet resilient and determined to smile through it all. Coming out the other side standing tall.

Growth Inhibited

When I got home things very quickly went back to their old patterns. Work, binge, purge, sleep repeat.

I couldn't fall back into the spiralling pit, so I made a decision. I cut ties completely with Simon and started making plans for myself.

Shirley Valentine had always been a favourite film of mine. I'd watched it with Mum on more than one occasion. I loved her sense of power in a situation where she felt unheard, unnoticed and unappreciated. I was going to be a Shirley. I was going to book a Europe tour. I had survived Ireland. I knew what backpacking life was like. I could handle it and I wanted more of that adventure. It was time to take on the role of *explorer* with the side dish of *travelling romance*.

Reckless acts aren't always destructive, and it sure beat the reckless act of bulimia. I couldn't inhibit my growth any longer the subservient role with Simon was cut from the performance. I needed to start living.

*

Months travelling meant that I had focus. I couldn't binge while in hostels and money was limited so I had to develop routines. Routines that felt safe and manageable.

I met Tom in Paris, my favourite city. The city of love, art, and pure beauty.

With the jaw-dropping lines of the glass pyramid at the Louvre, the breath-taking views from the top of the Eiffel Tower and the Arc de Triumph standing guard, laughing at the cars negotiating the star roundabout beneath.

The vibrant centre Pompidou filled with modern art, musicians busking and dance performances, enticing you into a frenzy of exuberance.

The majestic Notre Dame Cathedral winking through its huge rose windows, gothic architecture dissected with geometric rib vaults and spire reaching for the heavens with laser precision.

The perfect start to an exploration through the cities.

*

Rome came next. A bustling city of camera clad tourists scrambling through its desolate ruins.

The Coliseum, Roman Forum and Pantheon as statements of its history.

St Peter's Basilica watching down on the city in reverence and the square dotted with stalls selling gelato and miniature replicas of its icons.

Glamorous fountains as accents to its hidden streets, with piazzas highlighted by pizzerias omitting the sensual aromas of fresh dough, oregano and garlic.

Churches filled with Byzantine mosaics and beautiful stained glass leaving its multi-coloured imprints on the tiled floors below.

*

On to the Amalfi Coast, with pastel shades of delicate cafes weaving their way through labyrinths of alleyways, serving espressos, calamari and limoncello.

Soft sandy beaches, accented by turquoise water and lido decks dotted along the shore, promising bliss upon their whitewashed veneer. Lemon groves seducing you with their citrus scents.

*

Venice called. The city on the lagoon, serving an array of Venetian tapas to feast on in the golden hour of sunset.

As the sky turned vibrant fuchsia, cerise and tangerine, centre stage amongst the shadow blue curves of the gondolas, gliding smoothly and effortlessly along calm waters.

Life joining it and taking the opportunity to move at a slower pace.

*

Cycling around Prague with its ornate architecture, glass curved structures, baroque buildings in a palette of a hundred shades, gothic churches and medieval astronomical clock.

Pure white peacocks wandering around the grounds of the hilltop castle, museums filled with bohemian art and sunlight kissing the domes of churches all around.

An all you can eat buffet of sights and sounds.

A visit to the bone church in Kutna Horá with walls adorned with skulls, a haunting reminder of mortality.

*

Berlin bound. The city of contrasting highlights on its brow.

Remnants of the Berlin wall spattered with bullet holes and luminous graffiti as far as the eye can see.

Its TV Tower at Alexanderplatz standing like a guardian, angelic and strong.

Brandenburg Gate, with its crisp lines painted in the horizon and quadriga atop, riding through the clouds abreast.

A city of resilience. A city of art and culture, unashamed to stand out from the crowd.

*

Visits to Vienna. A city of music and dreams.

The Ring Strasse as its core. Walls towering above you, chiselled cheekbones and gargoyle jewellery.

History running through its bloodstream in waves.

Schnitzel, goulash and wine served on tablecloths of cotton.

The resplendent Hofburg palace carved out of icing with intricate detail and exquisite grandeur.

Renaissance architecture and bold street art.

*

Munich came last, punctuated by giant tankards of beer to dive into and pretzels the size of your head.

The Bavarian capital filled with cheer and freckled by chocolate brown lederhosen and electric blue dirndl.

The colour changing bubble of the Allianz arena sat playfully on its back waving its legs in the air like a ladybird.

The final stop of our tour.

"Prost!" Tom raised his glass, obscuring half of his body in the process with the caramel beer swimming inside.

"Prost!" I raised my glass of fresh orange. Not quite the same effect in a half-pint glass, but the sentiment remaining the same.

A celebratory cheer for the journey and the gratitude of having my private photographer travelling with me and documenting all the highlights.

I felt alive and free. In every city, I had experienced something different, met new people and gained confidence in myself.

I was stronger and more capable than I'd ever believed. Life felt good.

I would return home refreshed and with a sense of determination that I wouldn't go into the next decade struggling as much. I had wasted far too much time already and I had no idea how long I would have left to keep chancing fate.

I had absorbed the romance of Paris, the glamour of Italy, the resilience of Germany and the promise of Vienna.

I was to hold onto them like a sponge, heavy like cleansing holy water. I would need them. My struggles weren't quite over yet.

Reflection in Icy Waters

I made plans and started to look forward to the future. Tom would come to England and we would make a go of a relationship together here. We booked a trip to a Spanish villa with James, his new partner Sophie and another couple, Paula and Greg. One of the 'normal' things you do in relationships.

Little did I know that it was to be that Spanish holiday, that would truly break me open, like a frozen pond, buckled under pressure.

I hadn't anticipated how hard it would be to build a relationship based on the foundations of a travelling romance. When the day to day reality of Tom trying to find work, living with me 24/7 and struggling with depression all started to set in, things became tenser than stretched elastic.

"Have you done a job search today?" I would ask.

"Yeah, but nothing new on there. It'll be alright."

Would it? He had spent the day lounging around in my flat, cooking himself lunch from my cupboards and heating it with electricity I'd only topped up yesterday. I was manager of a therapy centre on the Wirral now, but certainly not bringing in enough to support two people.

"Maybe you could go to the job centre and they'll help you find something. You could do with anything really." I still wasn't very good at this assertive thing. I felt guilty immediately.

"Err, yeah. Right. I'll go tomorrow, ay."

Surely, he wanted to do something productive? He still had some of his savings left, but if he was going to settle in England, he'd want a career, wouldn't he? Being isolated in a flat, all day every day was never good for me, so I couldn't imagine it was good for him either.

*

The trip to Spain would be a welcome relief. I would be celebrating my 30th with great people around me.

Friends who had my back, or so I thought.

When we arrived at the villa it didn't take long for the atmosphere to shift. James and Sophie were all over each other constantly, like birds doing a mating dance. Paula and Greg were in their happily married bubble, and then there was me and Tom. Fractious and disconnected, resentment served as dressing. I felt completely alone.

“Let's go to the nature park to chill out today, yeah?” James was upbeat and radiant.

It was as if he was on a lovely holiday, relaxed and happy in his relationship.

I ran that thought through my head again. Hmm. Yes, thanks brain.

We packed our bags for the day, and all squeezed into the seven-seater silver hire car, like kids on a school trip. I was almost tempted to sing 99 bottles of beer on the wall, but I resisted.

We arrived at the nature park to a cocktail of scents in the air. Blood red carnations, baby piny orchids, and fuchsia lantanas all swaying and leaving trails of their perfume behind them like breadcrumbs. Fruit trees with arrays of oranges, lemons and limes like baubles on their branches. Glistening ponds with lily pads balanced atop, lush green helicopter pads for frogs to touch down. Butterflies dancing around to their private ballads.

Tom had wandered off on his own with his camera. Paparazzi to the fauna. I walked with James and Sophie.

“It was a great idea coming here, James.” I smiled. Nature lifted my spirits.

“It was my idea actually.” A sting from a scorpion’s tail. Sophie’s eyes sharp and unwavering.

“Oh. Ok. Well, great idea, Sophie.” I was trying here. Ever polite and engaging.

“We were going to come just the two of us, but James said to ask the rest of you. It’s a bit awkward with you and Tom though, isn’t it?!”

Was it? Was it that bad, that other people were noticing too?

“He’s a bit depressed, I think. We can’t all be loved up like you two I guess.” Oh my. That came out of my mouth before I could sugar coat it. The volcano was about to erupt.

“We are loved up yes. That’s normal when you are *actually* in love with someone and not just using them because you’ve got no-one better or going from one guy to the next. You probably need to stop clinging to James though, he has *me* now and doesn’t need you. I know you’re lonely, but he’s not yours anymore. I’m not even sure why you came on our holiday really?”

I was speechless, stunned, shocked. Briefly. But something had been triggered inside me. Maybe it was years of bullying and abuse, maybe it was because she was right. Whatever it was, a red mist descended, and I completely lost it.

"How dare you! Who do you think you are? I'm on this holiday because James paid for it as my birthday present. Yeah, you didn't know that did you? Because he was too scared to tell you. You sad spiteful cow! You think you're better than everyone, but you're not. People just feel sorry for you!"

I was a threatened lioness on the attack. My voice getting louder and louder with rage. James would stand up in my defence though, right? Tell her the truth? Tell her that he cared as much for me as he did for her?

He was stood between us like a defence shield, but I started to realise he wasn't protecting me. He was protecting her. The look of disappointment on his face scribed in permanent marker. How could I have told Sophie that?

This was his first serious relationship since our own, and the first time someone loved him back as ferociously as he loved them. He wasn't about to lose that for a fourteen-year friendship with an erratic, and now aggressive woman like me.

Sophie was in tears and had sat on a bench with Paula, safe under her wing.

"We'd better go back to the villa. I think everyone needs to calm down."

James' tone had a funeral speech, edge to it. There would be a period of mourning coming soon. The car journey back to the villa filled with lead silence, deafening and cold.

*

We all went off to our respective rooms and I hid in the bathroom, splashing water on my face to try and wash away the nasty woman I had become. Tom was nowhere to be found when I came out.

I knocked on Paula's door.

"Have you seen Tom? He's not in the villa."

"No. Have you tried ringing him?" She was still deflated and angry after everyone's day of fun had been cut short because of me and my outburst.

His mobile rang out. I tried four times. Nothing. I began to worry. He had told me previously that he would disappear for days and had lost so many friendships because people 'just couldn't handle him'.

This was to be my first trial.

Finally, my mobile rang.

"Tom, where are you?" I tried to remain calm, but my voice was jagged.

"I'm on the motorway. I can't do this anymore. I know you love James, not me. I'm useless and a waste of space."

"You need to come back. We need to talk about this properly. Tell me where you are exactly, and Greg can come to get you."

He gave me the nearest junction and I asked him to wait where he was.

"I think Tom is going to jump in the road. He's on the motorway and says he can't do it anymore."

I was pleading to Greg more than Paula. Paula had already made up her mind about me. Greg was a bit more lenient.

"We'll go and get him. You're best staying here."

"I'll come with you." James stepped up.

"So will I." Paula always had to be involved. The overseer of events.

Sophie was having a nap 'recovering from the day's events.'

"We'll be back as soon as we can."

*

The police had arrested Tom for walking down the hard shoulder. It was up to one of his rescuers to pay a fine for him to be released. Which of course meant Paula would step up with her card to further highlight how I'd caused her such grief.

*

Sophie also took the opportunity to seal the nail in my coffin in their absence.

I'd gone to knock on her door to apologise.

"Are you ok, Sophie? I was out of line earlier and I'm sorry. It's been a crazy time with things with Tom and I shouldn't have taken it out on you." No response.

The front door key turned, and I heard her leap up out of bed, opening her bedroom door in cheetah sprint, then bursting into tears.

"Get away from me, you psycho cow!"

Erm, what?

"James, get her away from me." She grabbed her arm with vice pressure, leaving a bright red mark in its wake. She already had a scratch down her face, that wasn't there when she had gone for her nap. There was a strange glint in her eye as she then went on to hit herself in the face near the graze.

I stood there motionless, watching a horror movie and waiting for it to finish, waiting for the killer to be caught.

James bounded up the stairs and dug past me as if I was undergrowth in the jungle.

"What happened?" He was flustered and already at breaking point from dealing with Spanish police and a suicidal burden.

Sophie wailed. "She attacked me, saying I should be the one on the motorway. That you were hers and that I needed to go!"

Even I believed her script and her frenzy.

James' face turned to me in robotic agony. Sadness, despair, rage and hurt beaming out of every pore.

"I think you should go."

"That's not what happened! I've been in my room crying, and only came to say sorry!"

Met with a stone stare, the judge and jury had already made their decision, I was to be found guilty without trial.

"If you get your bags together Paula and I will take you both to the airport first thing. Everyone needs sleep tonight, so I suggest you go and make sure Tom doesn't go running off anywhere again."

He embraced Sophie with angelic protection. She looked at me once more in pity. She had won and it was time I surrendered to my fate.

*

I was being sent home, on the holiday that was supposed to be celebrating making it this far in my life. The irony that I didn't see any future life ahead after this moment wasn't lost on me.

It would be the last I would hear from James for years. I was completely destroyed. I had flown from the nest of my mother into the nest of James, and now I'd been seemingly thrown out of both, and expected to fly.

The argument with Sophie had been far from the highlight of my life, but it was a symbol about how much the friendship with James had meant to me. It was stability amidst the chaos, security in the broken relationships and a safety net to me.

Now I needed to go through all that alone.

*

I asked Tom to leave. He would have to sort himself out from now on. I didn't want to look at him. It was easy to blame him for what had happened. Easier than me owning up to what I'd said in retaliation for having my co-dependency taken away.

Travelling romance very rarely works when you stand still, and the explorer inside me had long since left with the monotony of life.

He stayed in England for a long while, but very quickly blocked me from his life. He had met friends through me and was happy to go out and forget about me as if I was the blotch stain on his shirt that could be covered over with a suit jacket.

I never thought I would rebuild from that point of my life. My reflection looking back at me wasn't the woman I thought it was, but I did rebuild. Somehow.

Seeds Stay Dormant

I distracted myself by going back to my bucket list. I had to keep the momentum of overcoming my limiting beliefs and facing any fears going. Each challenge I faced built my confidence further, and right then I needed that boost.

Number four - Snowboarding.

It seemed to look so much easier than skiing, and so much cooler, but was equally as tough.

It was a reminder that my fitness levels were on a par with an eight - year old who had been housebound for several years. Several times I missed being able to jump onto the ski lift because I couldn't hop on in time.

Of course, you didn't just have the self-humiliation of not being able to do it, no! The whole ride would stop with an alarm going off, designed to prevent someone from getting bowled over by the rider behind, but in reality, a musical symphony mocking my inadequacy. The boarders in front of me wondering if they'd ever make it to the top, I'm sure.

When I did make it on the tiny round black disc, wobbling on the end of the stick, it was a small triumph in its own right. Like balancing plates, I had to get the momentum spot on. It carried me to the peak of the indoor piste and I would have free reign to descend again. The soft white dust beneath the foot, allowing you to glide and flow with snake-like grace, leaving you wishing for an endless mountain. I suddenly understood the thrill-seekers' buzz and wanted more of it.

*

Next up would be *number five, sky diving.*

I was still terrified of heights, but I gathered together a group of friends to jump with me, and there felt like safety in numbers.

"Are we mad?" One of my friends Neil asked.

"Of course we are!" I joked. My stomach doing somersaults in Olympic fashion. "But think of how amazing you will feel when you land!"

We were jumbled together in groups onto a plane the size of a handcrafted model. I'm pretty sure I saw some duct tape holding the wing on.

What was I doing? Whose idea was this? Maybe I could sidle off to the side and say I had stomach cramps or something? A memory of PE class came back to me. Finding excuses not to join in as a result of never feeling good enough.

Not this time you! No more excuses! Deep breath. Let's do this!

*

"Remember chin to chest as you leave the plane. I will ease you to the edge and you will sit with your legs on the side of the plane as I count you out." We had already been debriefed, but I appreciated the reminder.

One by one I watched my three friends each sit in the opening of the plane. There one minute and gone the next. Then it was my turn.

My instructor Eddie gradually shuffled me into the doorway, like a dead-weight child not wanting to go to school. I could feel the wind rushing past my face with force. Chin down. Chin down. Chin down.

"3, 2, 1"

We were falling. The air pushing my whole-body weight upwards and juggling my skin like pizza dough. The freefall was over in less than a minute before the chute opened, but an exhilaration like no other.

Then the real magic followed. Floating in the sky, like a dandelion seed, no sound, weightless, free. I could have stayed up there above the clouds forever.

Nothing to think about, nowhere to be, no-one to answer to, just the sun on the horizon and the patchwork fields below. It's not a feeling that could ever be replicated, but it is one that shifted my perspective completely.

The dots below running around, all in their mini worlds, interconnected, yet separate. Some of them oblivious to the fact I was even up in the sky above them. It brought home how insignificant we all are.

How egotistical I had been to think that anyone even cared about what life choices I make, who I am or where I've come from. Yes, my closest family and friends might have a say, but in the grand scheme of things, I was merely a grain of sand in a whole expanse of desert. I needed to start thinking about me, what I wanted to achieve, how I wanted to better myself each day.

The pure adrenaline rush after landing back on the earth was euphoric. I felt invincible, like I could achieve anything.

It took me back to a time at school when we had done abseiling and I had thought there was no chance that I would be able to ever lean back off that cliff. Who in their right minds does that? Yet there I was walking down the craggy rocks, shaking in fear, still taking those tiny steps and holding back the tears with every drop of pride I could squeeze out.

I learned quite quickly that feeling the fear and doing it anyway switches something in your brain. You suddenly get the urge to push yourself even further, to try more, to step out of your comfort zone. I knew why adrenaline junkies get seemingly crazier and crazier ideas about what they will try next. It's about pushing boundaries and pushing limits.

I didn't need to do anything more daring immediately following that. It was enough to know that I could challenge myself, feel terrified, yet still overcome that.

Those dormant seeds of courage being nurtured.

A State of Deep Rest

I joined an online dating site for an ego boost. I didn't want another relationship, but I needed to know that someone could desire me. That I wasn't a spent hag ready for the scrap heap.

*

I met a funny musician called Jackson. We agreed to meet up as friends for a drink. I 'definitely didn't want anything serious' and he respected that. From the minute we met my face ached from laughing and smiling. His humour was witty, quick and wacky. We were going to get on great.

We met up a few times and when we met for a movie at his flat, I knew he was the rest and healing I needed. I didn't have to play a role this time. His arms were open without motive or demand. I could just breathe for a short while.

"I never want to leave here." I didn't.

"Then don't." His words like liquid silk washing over my heart, encasing it in sanctuary and hope. We melted into each other's arms. Romeo and Juliet entwined in a lover's embrace.

Jackson joined me on my second skydive. He brought the adventure and fun to my life that I had craved in my core, but never truly nourished. I wanted to share every experience with him.

*

We went back to Ireland together, and ticked off another point on my bucket list by crossing a rope bridge. Something that the vertigo I'd inherited as part of my collective ME symptoms prevented me from doing without chronic nausea, or the feeling of wanting to jump.

This was one of the hardest and one that I've been unable to replicate since, but I did it, and the satisfaction in that is as rewarding as a cold tile floor on a baking hot day.

Jackson truly loved me. There was no malice in his bones, and I fell into his arms like a child into a beanbag. For the first time since my relationship had broken down with James, I felt cared for and supported, without expectation.

With my branches and trunk exposed in wintery light, he still only saw the beauty of my silhouette. There was such strength in his belief in me. This was it. This was hope. This was trust. This was freedom.

I had to finally let go of the ties that were pulling me back. I couldn't hold in my truths anymore. I needed to start living out my dreams, building my confidence further and ditching habits that no longer served me.

I would start following my instincts more. I had nothing to lose. On more than one occasion I had doubted my gut, and I had ended up regretting it, so moving forward I would trust what it was telling me and listen.

Roots Anchored

I was dancing several nights a week at that point. I loved the feeling of release it brought. The beat of the music and the palanquin notes carrying me across the floor. I had nowhere else to be, and nothing else to think about, other than the flow of symphony running through my body, transporting me into a timeless bliss.

I met a charismatic dancer called Sean and he snatched me for as many dances as he could. He was a great dancer, slick like oil, with snake hips, and his smile lit up the room with confident charm. He held my hand like it was precious crystal, the lightest touch, enough to connect the energy between us. We would glide across the floor in complete synergy. Fred Astaire and Ginger Rogers.

"I've seen you on Facebook." I wasn't sure if that was a good thing, but he was still smiling, so maybe I was safe on that one. "I've wanted to say hi properly for ages. Where else do you dance?"

"Everywhere I can," I joked.

It really was my latest elixir. The nights I didn't dance left me feeling quite deflated. I should have felt content with Jackson, but he had his own life separate from me. He was in a band who practised or played throughout the week, so dancing was the filler of the gap, far better than sitting home alone.

The compliments I received from other dancers, and the fact people picked me to dance with, were all the reassurance I needed. After years of being picked last and not feeling good enough, this was my moment to shine.

"Maybe I'll come to join you. I need to get back into dancing more. I used to dance every night of the week." Sean was keen and passionate.

My kind of guy.

Did I just think that aloud? What about Jackson?

It's only dancing, chill.

We started travelling to different venues together. Sean would pick me up and drop me back home. I loved his company. He was charismatic and witty and there was a huge spark connecting us.

Weeks in I realised that this was no longer just dancing. I had to draw a close on my relationship with Jackson. This was the time my intuition would speak to me and I would listen. I couldn't continue in a relationship with someone knowing I had feelings for someone else.

I would break Jackson's heart, but I had to trust my own. I loved him, but my branches were following the light elsewhere.

*

It wasn't long before I was living with Sean and we were going on our own adventures.

People told us that we were rushing into things and that it was a whirlwind romance that wouldn't last, but it was never whirlwind for us. We loved each other deeply, and our relationship felt like home.

My roots were becoming anchored and I finally thought I'd found my place in the forest and my leading role.

Decline of Darkness Begins

Within a year we were married. Within another year we had our first child, and that was when the reality of life set in. I was now *dutiful wife* and *mother.*

Nothing can prepare you for motherhood. For the sheer exhaustion, the self-doubt, the guilt, the fear, the responsibility, or the joy. From the moment that baby is in your arms, you experience love like you've never felt before. This mini human is completely dependent on you to keep them alive and to keep them safe.

I think a situation like that can either make someone or break them. Thankfully it was to make me. Not in a linear, straight forward, easy, epiphany fashion, but in a gradual realisation that some things I was still clinging to weren't going to wash anymore.

I was a mum. This was an opportunity that I had been told would never be possible. Like the fact I wouldn't make it past thirty, here I was proving doctors wrong once again, and I needed to embrace it with everything I had. No matter what the cost.

I had to teach my daughter values and beliefs.

That would mean *trusting* my values and beliefs and starting to shape them into something that I would want to pass down the generations. I couldn't teach self-respect, self-care, boundaries and going for your dreams if I wasn't reaching for the stars myself.

I couldn't tell her how sacred her body was and how incredible a human she was, if I was still periodically binging and purging or looking in the mirror with disgust.

This part was the making of me. This was an act that never felt like an act, but a natural desire that had been suppressed and one that filled me with the passion to keep returning for an encore.

The marriage was secondary to that. I always thought I would feel of worth once I'd met 'the one.' Goodness knows I'd tried to play every role to get that. It wasn't the marriage that saved me. Sean wasn't my knight in shining armour.

What saved me from myself was the role of being a mother, but not just a mother to my children, a mother to myself.

The winter of my life would be a time of healing, nurturing and nourishment, from me to me.

It was going to be a bumpy ride though.

I was ill during pregnancy with hyperemesis gravida. After twenty-six weeks I had to give up working because I was too nauseous to be of any use. I spent the whole nine months in and out of the hospital, and I felt useless and depressed. I joined some local mums' groups, but the strain started to build in my relationship with Sean and light started to shine on the hairline cracks that were there.

I didn't look ill and I wouldn't ask for help when I needed it. I would push through it, then complain about how I felt overwhelmed and taken for granted. I was my own worst enemy on more than one occasion.

*

"I think I want a home birth." I'd seen enough of hospitals and wanted to be in familiar surroundings, where I felt at ease and comfortable.

"I don't like the sound of that. What if something goes wrong? It's dangerous." Sean's words came out, but they didn't go into my ears.

"I've already booked for the one to one midwives to come around. I've got a DVD if you want to watch it?" I thrust the plastic box into his hands. The decision had already been made. It was *my* body and it was up to *me*.

It was our first big decision to negotiate and the first time that it was clear he didn't have an option in it all.

When my mind was made up on something, he would have to go along with it for the sake of less argument.

*

We had several differences. I was a vegetarian and he was a meat-eater. I was interested in more natural parenting, like breastfeeding, co-sleeping, home schooling and holistic medicine. He was old school parenting, so felt out of his comfort zone with anything different. I was an early riser who liked to get things done first thing, then go to bed early. He was a night owl who liked to stay up and binge watch episodes of the latest series that was out. I liked my own space and was content visiting other people. He wanted to invite people to us.

Our differences hadn't been an issue, but when there was another dependent thrown into the mix, they became a reason for resentment to form and became like cancer within our marriage. I was no longer able to dance because of the sickness. Dancing was where we met, and it was where we both came alive, let go of our stress and connected. It was part of the bond that had held us together for the first eighteen months and it was beginning to lose its grip.

Sean had been off work with stress for a long while and we decided that when early retirement came up, he should take it and think about doing something different. He wasn't going to get this opportunity again, and watching his child grow up as much as possible was far more important to us both, than him working seventy hours a week for slightly more income. His family were concerned that it was irresponsible, but we trusted our choice so had to just go for it anyway.

He re-trained as a gym instructor and personal trainer and eventually caught lucky when we had visited a cafe we loved, and he had watched a sports class for kids.

"I want to work with kids, not adults." It was a lightbulb moment for him and his whole aura beamed. "I've spoken with the coach here and he's given me the details of the guy to ring. Is that ok?"

How could I say no? It was the perfect opportunity for him to let his comedic side out, to do something more active and to be involved in fitness but not stuck in a stuffy gym. I'd always said life was about following dreams and taking opportunities, so it was his turn to do the same.

"I think you should go for it, yes!"

Maybe our problems were there because he didn't feel like he was contributing while he was out of work. Maybe this would ease the pressure.

*

It worked well during my pregnancy, because of the sickness. I would go with him to classes and sit and read while he taught. It was part-time, so we got to spend significant time together and I got to see different parts of the country. Once our daughter was here, I continued to go with him, and spent time in cafes eating cake and enjoying maternity leave.

We loved spending as much time together as possible as a small family.

Our daughter became the cement that brought a lot of broken family pieces together. My dad and Liz made more effort to come over. Sean's family became more involved, and I felt I had more purpose.

I would go to mum's groups and meet other women who had similar parenting styles that I loved. Suddenly I fitted in somewhere that I hadn't previously. People looked forward to seeing me.

I decided to breastfeed and that was my sacred moment that no-one else could take my place for. My daughter needed me for that. Anyone else could cuddle her or play with her, but I was her source of food and I was overjoyed with that. In order to feed her I needed to look after my own body, so the binges stopped, and I made sure I had regular meals.

I stopped looking at my body with disdain and saw it as an incredible vessel that had both created life and was now sustaining it. I had way more lumpy bits, saggy bits and blobby bits, but it didn't matter. I had more worth now than my desirability.

*

I would wear her in a sling and hold her close. I saw the bond that my mum had with me, and must have had with my sister, Laura, before me. "I'm sorry I put you through such heart-breaking times, Mum. I didn't realise how painful that must have been to watch me in self-destruct."

We both had tears in our eyes and hearts wide open.

"The dark times are passing now, my love. You are a wonderful mother and I'm so proud of you."

I was proud of me too, and grateful, unbelievably grateful.

My dad saw Laura in my daughter too. It was the first time I'd seen him cry as we spoke about it. "She is the image of her. It takes me right back all those years. She's never been forgotten."

"I know, Dad. I know." I wondered who was doing the parenting now, as I reassured him that it was ok to be upset and that he had another chance to watch a child grow.

I had been given this chance of motherhood to heal a lot of hurts. I needed to let go of my sadness about him missing my childhood and allow him to embrace this opportunity.

The dark times were declining.

Hope Presents Itself

From the minute my daughter was born there were greater forces at work than I could control anymore. She looked to me as a role model and I wanted to be a good one.

The world didn't revolve around me anymore. Any choices I made had greater consequences and I had a sense of responsibility that would never leave.

Hope for a future had presented itself and I couldn't just brush that off. This was the start of a family that I never thought I'd have, and never could have imagined possible.

"I think I'd like another child." As the words came out of my mouth, I surprised myself just as much as Sean.

"Really? What if you're sick again?"

I hadn't thought about that. My hormones were raging like a storm through my body, and all sense of logic, reason or planning had gone out of the window.

"I'm sure I'll be fine. I'll take it easy this time and take early maternity. Maybe you'll get your little boy." I knew it was good bait after his two daughters before me and our own together, but manipulation wasn't on my radar either. It was time to use any tools I could find, regardless of how I would reflect on my actions later.

"We're gonna need a bigger house!" he joked.

I'll take that as a yes.

His now-teenage daughters were still sleeping in bunk beds in one room, while our daughter had her cot in her own room, so I agreed we would need more space. I wanted everyone to have their own space so that they felt part of the family, despite his girls only staying one night a week.

I trawled the internet for weeks looking for something bigger, but they were all out of our price bracket, until I finally thought about where I'd grown up as a child. My memories were rose-tinted with a high gloss filter. I had such fond recollections of walks along the prom, days on the beach and picnics in the park, that it felt like a positive move.

Was hope presenting itself again?

"I've found a five-bedroom house that's only forty pounds more than this one a month." Best beaming excited smile on now.

"Oh wow! Where's that?"

"Wallasey. Near where I grew up. I've booked a viewing for tomorrow." Once again, it wouldn't be me asking him for an opinion, it would be me answering for both of us and arranging all the details.

It could only be described as 'interesting' when the estate agent opened the door.

The carpets were wine red with paisley patterns swirling through them like a potato printing session at pre-school. The woodwork was varnished like dark chocolate and the walls decorated in shades of silvery black, racing car red and amethyst purple. There were mousetraps hidden in alcoves and under the stairs and there was a fragrance of cumin and coriander impregnated into every surface.

There were five bedrooms so plenty of room. It would need a lot of work, but for once, I saw potential in something. There were two toilets, so no more fighting on Saturday mornings and I could have one of the rooms downstairs to do my treatments in.

"I love the height of the ceilings, and the cornices are amazing. Our bedroom is huge, and we could have the new baby in the room right next to us. My brothers will help with decorating and we can go down to watch the ships go past with the kids."

I was reeling off everything positive I could think of. Sean looked apprehensive. I'd have to make this decision myself.

"I think we should go for it. They've said they'll put laminate flooring down and you could have your little office upstairs to do all your creative stuff you keep saying you want to try again, that you haven't done for years. The utility room will be ideal to store all your sports equipment in too. It will be perfect, trust me."

I was convincing myself as much as him. Having a bigger house would bring the dream of a bigger family closer to reality, and that felt like the answer to every question right now.

"Ok. Let's do it."

The Frost

We moved in September and by the January I was being sick each morning. There was no hiding pregnancy until the twelve-week mark for me.

The hyperemesis started as soon as the hormones kicked in. We were going to have another baby in October. Things were falling into place. I was building the family that I never dreamt was possible for me.

That's the thing about dreams though. They can change within a minute.

This dream was not the one that was going to leave me waking up in bliss state. The surprise frost was to come.

Eleven weeks in I felt less nausea and stopped being sick. Something was different. I rang my midwife and we booked an ultrasound.

We went for the scan and I knew before any words were uttered that this life was gone. The silence in the room hung like lead clouds. The formed cells were still there, floating inside me, but there was no longer a heartbeat. No further growth to happen. A lifeless body inside a body that would ache to trade places.

I already knew. I already felt it. The sickness had eased days before, but I needed them to keep checking that there was nothing to see. That they were sure this fantasy had been smashed into a million pieces of lost hope.

They were sure. I was empty, yet still full. The process had begun, and over the coming week I would bleed out all the plans we'd made and the visions of our family complete.

I didn't cry in that room. They had seen this dozens of times before. They had given the same news to so many women, shattering their hearts, that I felt stupid even thinking I was anything special, or anyone to comfort in such tragedy. My mum had been through this and worse, over and over.

I had to acknowledge that nature had made its choice and get on with it. My suffering was nothing compared to others. How could I even begin to feel sorry for myself? The walls had come up, disassociate from it all, numb it out, self-protect. Don't allow yourself to feel. Stay in control.

The problem with building walls around yourself with brittle foundations of reason behind them is that at some point they will crash down with a bang. I already knew this, but the tears would have to wait.

The whole situation was just matter of fact and I would have to let it run its course.

I wasn't prepared for what was to follow.

*

Friends who had been through the process had told me there would be pain. Think of period pain, and it would be like that, they said. It was not similar. Hammers pounded me in my lower abdomen. My insides twisted into a knotted balloon knot, and my muscle fibres were torn apart like fresh bread. Breaking me open.

I couldn't lie down because the pressure was worse, a shaken pop bottle waiting to burst. Rolling around with a hot water bottle, curling up in a ball, wrenching and agonised. I didn't want this to happen. I was clinging on to what was left inside me. Letting go would be admitting it was no more. I wasn't ready, but I had no option this time.

Standing up I would go faint with the pain. The only choice left was to lock the bathroom door and allow the ritual to unfold. I ran a bath. No bubbles this time. There would be no joy in this submersion. This was a cleansing, but no soap would be needed, no perfume. I had already bled clots of ended life away, but I knew it wasn't quite over yet, and there was still more to come. The contractions were still gripping my womb, forcing me to release, to be present in this moment and witness the whole experience.

I lay in the bath for what felt like hours. The water crimson and cursed. Rooted in the pain of it. The tears no longer able to be repressed. Flooding out of me in torrents.

I suffered alongside all the mothers who had lost before me, and who were to lose again after me. I suffered with those who have never had the chance for a seed to ripen within them. I suffered with those who had birthed a child only for them to be lost too young.

There is no hierarchy of pain. I was as valid as any other. This was my loss, and it was as devastating as any other loss. My body shaking, tribal moans, with tears streaming, frozen in time. In a moment of grief, release, exhaustion.

I wept for all the days that I'd held it together for other people. I wept for the plans we'd made. I wept for getting caught up in the excitement and telling so many people about the pregnancy, before that iron-clad twelve-week mark. I wept for the friends who had been through this and more. I wept for the gratitude of birthing a healthy child years before. I wept for my naivety that this could never happen to me, because I had already been through a viable pregnancy. I wept for the sickness I had hated and wished away. I wept for the thought of October coming and having no bundle of joy to hold.

The tears fell in the scarlet water until I was empty, lighter, purged.

I got out of the bath knowing that from that moment on there would be a deeper sense of gratitude for everything I had, and every experience I was yet to feel. When the pain had become too much to bear, and I couldn't control the outcome, all I could do was surrender and hand it over to a greater force. That was a bittersweet lesson to learn.

I had always thought surrendering was about being weak, that it made you vulnerable, that it made you open to attack. At that moment though, sobbing in that white cocoon turned red, I realised that surrendering takes an enormous amount of bravery and acceptance. When you realise that there is absolutely nothing more you can do within a situation and can accept that, therein lies your liberation.

We often assume we will live forever, that every life will go on, but life never works that way. I reflected on my mum telling me how she had lost several pregnancies. It shocked me how she had got through that experience repeatedly, and lost a child after birth, yet still went on to have me and my brothers.

It was a stark reminder of how powerful the human spirit can be under adversity. Through the storms of life, some lives are not destined to live long. They come in, shine brightly and leave lasting imprints within other hearts. Like tree blossom, not all of them will ripen into fruit, and reach the potential of others, yet they all have their space upon the branches of life.

Comfort and Celebration

It was only a month later I was being sick again. I took a test and the faint pink line winked at me. Torment and joy in two parallel vertices. How could I go through it again? How cruel was life going to be to me? This was going to be the longest nine months of my life and I didn't even know the half of it.

Because my hormones had not had a chance to reset after the miscarriage, I would be sicker than ever before, unable to hold down my own saliva, and constantly feeling like I was on a ship with nausea. I would lose two stone. My hair would fall out, and I would spend most of the year in and out of hospital on drips, being monitored and given cocktails of anti-sickness drugs.

It was a cruel joke. I had fought anorexia-bulimia for years and had started to win, only to face sickness out of my control. My body playing games with me again.

*

"Something's happening. I'm getting pains every few minutes. You'd best call the midwife." I was doubled over the bed and struggling to breathe, let alone speak.

"You're only twenty-six weeks, aren't you?" Sean had turned pale.

It was bonfire night and only a matter of days since our lost child had been due. It felt like some twisted trick to be going into labour now.

Within an hour I was at the hospital with midwives and doctors scurrying around.

"We need to give you some medication to stop the contractions, and a steroid injection for the baby in case you deliver today."

Deliver today?

"I don't mind delivering today!" I was in an exhausted and delirious state and wanted this torture from my body to end.

"If your baby is born now, they will have to go to neonatal, darling." I could tell she was trying to warn me about something serious. She had that schoolteacher manner about her voice, but I couldn't conceive how tiny my little boy would be, and I was happy for the pregnancy to be over and the nausea to subside.

"Ok. Do what you have to for the baby to be safe." I had to surrender again. My body was not my own and I had little authority of what would happen to it.

They stabilised my contractions and active labour stopped. I would have ten more weeks of sickness, contractions, false labours and being imprisoned in my own skin to endure yet.

The hospital wanted to induce me at 37 weeks. I was terrified, but thankfully this fear would be bypassed.

My waters broke at 3 am on 36 +6 days. We drove to the hospital and I got into a kneeling position on the bed with my hypnobirthing mp3 playing in my ears. I zoned out and let my body do its thing. I couldn't control my body, but I could control how I was going to deal with it.

*

"We need to move you to another room I'm afraid. There's no space on the ward yet and we need the delivery room."

We were escorted to another room, baby in arms and still aching from the delivery. It was like being placed in a storage fridge.

"Have you got any spare blankets at all?" My teeth chattered as I asked.

"I'll see what I can do." The midwife looked frazzled, and there was an alarm going off in the hallway, with doctors rushing around like a school breaktime bell.

Our son was still squished up with eyes closed. He hadn't fed yet and I was starting to worry.

"He won't latch, he keeps falling asleep." This wasn't like my first experience at all.

The benchmarks I'd set in my head for what birthing and motherhood should look like were already set by my daughter.

Our son was using all his energy to stay warm, so had no energy left to feed properly. There were to be several days of him being separated from me in a cot warmer, fed with formula and me feeling like I'd failed him as a mother. It was a compromise that felt beyond challenging.

The only joy I took from those few days, was that I was permitted rest and time to bond when I could finally feed him myself. I knew when I returned home, life would be back to normal. I would run the house, look after two children and Sean, and there would be very little rest between.

So, I made the most of that sacred seventy-two hours, even with every check-up and interruption, it was a time of comfort and solitary celebration that I had survived another trial.

Bare and Exposed

We got home and soon things tried to claw their way into a new routine. A baby to feed and change, minimal sleep, a toddler to entertain and ensure didn't feel left out, a house to clean, meals to cook and a husband to care for. The juggling act had begun again, except this time there were more balls to juggle and the added part of the trick was me still suffering from regular sickness.

"You need to go back to the doctor."

"Last time I went they said it was probably hormone related because of the breastfeeding."

"Well you've stopped feeding now and it's been eighteen months. You shouldn't still be being sick." Sean was right, but I was reluctant. I had been poked and prodded so many times each time I visited the GP, and had blood test after blood test, sometimes with inflammation markers high, then back in the normal range, each time with a different face to explain my story to once more. I was beginning to think I was a hypochondriac and there was nothing wrong with me. I was in a constant state of exhaustion though and things were only about to get harder now our son was walking too.

"Ok, I'll make an appointment for later."

*

The waiting room was stuffy and filled with coughing splutters in each corner. Posters on the wall mentioning the flu jab had corners curling up like a duck's tail, with faded writing and a dozen pinholes in them from various relocation attempts. We sat along the benches around the edge of the room, each avoiding eye contact with the drunk who sat at the end mumbling to himself, picking his fingers and giving off an aroma of ammonia and whiskey.

The blue screen flashed up names, with an electronic voice interpreting what it said. I was waiting for a tricky name to pop up for entertainment value, but the computer got each one right this time and it was soon my own name across the screen. "Room 2." Ok here goes.

"So, you have had nausea and vomiting since your little boy was born eighteen months ago?"

"Yes, pretty much."

"Any blood or stomach cramps?"

"Sometimes, yes."

"Can I look at your stomach? If you pop yourself up on the couch, I will have a feel."

Standard procedure now, and one I was used to. I resumed my normal position while cold hands circled my abdomen, applying pressure in various places and asking, "Any pain here?"

"It's tender there, yes."

"Hmm, well pop off the couch and we'll get your weight and blood pressure."

I didn't look at the scales. Years ago, I would have delighted in seeing the needle hover over such a low number, but it was debilitating this time, and I didn't feel euphoric and slim.

"I think we need to do some more tests. I can see you've had several blood tests, but I'd like to send you for an endoscopy and an ultrasound, then we can go from there. Is that ok?"

I had an endoscopy as a teenager when I was losing weight drastically and they couldn't figure out why. My recollection was not a great one. I remember going into panic as soon as the camera hit my throat, coughing and retching. The doctor at the time had zero patience and rasped at me to calm down. Tears streaming down my face, I had eventually relaxed enough for him to perform the act. It wasn't the first time I had been violated and it wasn't the last.

Although I was filled with dread at the thought of it, all other tests had drawn a blank and it was either this or a barium meal. So, the camera felt the less terrifying prospect.

"That's ok, yes."

*

I had an appointment through for the procedure after a couple of weeks. I walked through the familiar hospital doors, welcoming me back like an old friend that you wished you'd not been back in touch with.

The staff in the department were very reassuring though, with big smiles on their face and warmth as they greeted me.

"We'll look after you today, don't worry. You won't be waiting long, and we'll talk you through it." They obviously saw the blind panic written all over my face from freckle to freckle.

It was a complete contrast to my first experience. I was guided into a chair and tilted back like I was at the dentist. There was an image of a tropical beach on the ceiling and I focused on it with deep intent. Thumbnails pressed into the palm of my hand as a further distraction.

There were a couple of mumbles and technical words passed between the doctors and they called for further advice. They would take a biopsy sample of some polyps they found and further reassure me it was just routine. The whole experience felt like it was over in seconds. Relief washed over me like a summer shower. Now I had to wait for my results.

I wasn't sure what polyps were, but they weren't gasping at the sight of the images on the screen, so I took that as a positive sign. Maybe the sickness was stress or hormones fighting to get back to normal after all.

*

The wind was about to be taken from my sails around a week later, when I received a call from the GP.

"We need to make an appointment for you to come and discuss your results."

My heart sank like concrete boots to the bottom of my watery existence.

"I can come today after twelve?"

"I've booked that for you at ten past one."

Ok, so maybe it wasn't all bad. Maybe it was another one of those times when the results were all clear and it was on to the next test.

I sat down in the doctor's chair and awaited the verdict.

"So, you had a biopsy taken when they did the endoscopy, and it has shown up changed cells. They are pre-cancerous and nothing to be alarmed about, but I can give you some medication and then come back in a couple of months to see if things have improved."

I was speechless. How could I not be alarmed about changed cells? Pre-cancerous cells? That's not normal cells. That's the step before cancer. I had been here before and last time they had laser blasted the offending parties away. This time I was just supposed to take a couple of pills to stop my body producing as much acid and pills to counteract the side effects of them.

The ultrasound seemed pointless now. I had already been given my sentence, but I would have to follow the procedure this time. My body an alien to me once more.

It was another wake-up call.

Years of abuse to my body had led me to this point. My body had taken enough battering and it was spent. I was lucky to be sat there, yet there were still massive changes I needed to make. I had been allowed to be a mum, despite all the odds stacked against me. I wasn't about to lose all that and miss out on watching them grow up. I had to find solutions. I had to treat my body with respect now, and I had to do everything I could to ward off any bigger problems creeping in.

I was bare and exposed to the elements, but I had armour to call upon. The motivation for change was there.

Strong and Immortal

I agreed to try the medication but asked for a fortnight's grace to see if I could find any other solutions to help with my symptoms. The GP agreed and I would come back for review a few months later.

I had already studied how the body relates to the mind and how emotions could be stored in our body and cause dis-ease. I had to know if all the resentment, anger and hurt of the previous years had partly brought me here. I could no longer welcome the thought of checking out early. I had two children to think about. I had to do whatever it took to try and reverse the cycle of deterioration I'd put my body through.

Memories of a million voices amplified in my mind, mocking me, telling me I was worthless, telling me I would never see past my third decade. Echoes of my past tormenting me and taunting me, screaming for me to give up this time.

I had to find solid ground again, remember the courage that had already got me this far, stand strong, and finally let go of those last leaves tainting my branches. The old beliefs and patterns of conditioning.

All I could do was to try my hardest. I had a sense of peace knowing that if I gave it 110% and the outcome still wasn't great, then I would have known I could do no more.

*

I studied everything I could on healthy living. Diet, lifestyle, household products. I wanted to know it all. I had to include stress reduction in my life. Meditation, yoga, breathing. I also needed to shift my diet from processed foods to whole foods for optimum nutrition. A good friend recommended a raw fruit and veg diet, to put less strain on my digestive system, so I decided to give it a go and see how things went from there.

Within a matter of days, my symptoms subsided. The nausea was fleeting, I was no longer being sick and for the first time in a long time my eyes weren't sunken and grey. I set myself a target of one-month high raw foods and then I'd go from there.

Six months in I'd forgotten that it was just a trial, and when I returned to the GP, they were delighted to see me looking so well.

I wasn't naive in thinking that I'd cured all my ailments, but if I had bought myself a bit more time, then that was enough for me. That was worth being so different to other people, worth having to answer the questions about the huge amounts of fruit and veg I was eating, of declining invitations to go out for meals and of shifting my body clock so I was up earlier to do meditation and yoga, then in bed earlier to ensure I had enough sleep.

I have always felt different, so actually being different didn't affect me too much.

*

While I wouldn't recommend everyone choosing the same therapeutic methods as I had, this was the right method for me at that time.

It had taken everything I had ever studied and read over my life to get myself through those first few months, but somehow, I had done it. I am under no illusion how fortunate I was to begin to strengthen broken roots again but strengthen I did.

I don't think you can go through periods of illness and recovery, without developing a deep appreciation for the gift of your life. Gratitude became a daily practice for me from that point onwards. I realised that even the darkest days had lessons to be learned and I had to live each day to the full.

I started to build up vigour again and my energy levels improved tenfold.

We settled into a new routine as a family, and things were gliding along across the ice, with just hairline cracks beneath the surface. I hadn't realised that I was yet to face a blizzard that would cover my world in a blanket of snow and leave me having to find a new course to follow.

I was to be reminded that we are not immortal, despite overcoming the odds several times.

Blood Red Holly

My dad was poorly. We had received the same text a few times before, how he had taken ill, it may be cancer, they are doing tests. Except this time the boy really was crying wolf.

He was in intensive care. We were to rush to see him in case he didn't make it through the night.

Guilt swept over me in a sandstorm cloud. I should have gone over to visit him more. I should have made more effort. We had been through the years of bitterness and resentment. We had healed a lot of pain. I should have made the most of that relationship we had developed. I might have lost my chance now and the regret was palpable.

*

The doctors couldn't establish what was wrong. There were contradictions in diagnosis, and he was currently on life support and asleep. It would be the first episode in a series of confusion, tests, hope, fear, more tests, relief, disappointment and further hospital admissions. I made a conscious decision when he pulled through that first time that I would make more effort. That Christmas he was allowed home might well have been his last, so I would go over with the kids and show him how loved he was.

He was frail. He didn't look like my dad anymore. He was wearing my grandad's face and ageing by the minute. His skin was grey. He couldn't eat and was short of breath. The only blessing was that he had finally given up smoking, after what must have been fifty years of tobacco-stained fingers and a raspy cough.

The kids were oblivious to his ailments. They bounced on his knees. Innocent, loving perfection. I saw him smile and I locked the memory of it deep in my heart. He knew this might be his last Christmas too, and he was relishing every moment of it, clearing away the years of abandonment we both felt, through his grandchildren.

Transforming the loss of his first daughter and embracing the achievements of his second.

That would be the last time I saw that smile. If I could have bottled that moment, I would have done in a heartbeat.

*

The weeks that followed were exhausting emotionally, physically and mentally. He was rushed back into the hospital. There were issues with his leg, and he was getting pains in his chest. I took the kids to visit him to try and cheer him up, but he was too drowsy from the medication, so the next few times I went alone.

He was transferred to a different hospital. Liz could no longer get there, as it was too far to travel. She didn't drive and collecting her from Runcorn and driving a 52-mile round trip for her to be at her husband's bedside was impossible between my own family duties. No-one else stepped up to be her chauffeur either, so I couldn't carry all the guilt for that.

Dad didn't want to be alone and my brothers were in work, so it was down to me to go to him. When I arrived, he was in an emergency department in a side room, waiting for a bed. He was scared. He was confused.

I no longer saw any of the hurt I'd felt over the years. I saw a young boy in a grown man's body. The fragile little child that had once trusted the world and loved without reason. His actions that I'd felt so angry about in previous years melted away. He had been hurt too. He had struggled to find a way through the battles of life.

He was imperfect. He had faced disappointment at how life had turned out differently than he'd planned. His trust had been broken. He had brought me into this world, unsure how to be a father and hadn't always got it right, but he loved me and now he needed me to love him back.

*

I didn't know how to do this. To watch someone, die. His leg was swollen and black. He had tubes coming from various veins, could no longer walk, and his spirit was flagging. He would be admitted for a matter of weeks, always asking when he could go home, always complaining that he hated hospitals.

"So do I, Dad, so do I. This is the best place for you right now though, and they will take care of you."

"The food is disgusting; can't you bring me in a bacon buttie?"

I wished I could. I wished I could fulfil his every wish in those moments.

"Sorry, Dad, but no. You can't have anything too salty now. I've brought you in some of your favourite music to play, ok?"

He switched his TV back to Judge Rinder and zoned back out. A moody teenager.

His kidneys were failing, and I was pulled aside by a doctor into his office.

"We have tried to stabilise his kidneys, but they're not responding. At some point, we need to stop supporting him, but we need permission from his next of kin."

Bang. My head exploded. My chest erupted. My stomach lurched. What was he saying? That he needed permission to let my dad die? Who could say yes to that?

No! I'm not going to permit that. It's too soon. I need more time. There are things I need to tell him. Things he needs to know.

I rang Liz. She couldn't make that decision or give consent either; she was too heartbroken. So, the card of fate was passed back to me.

Deep breaths. Please, universe give me a sign. Give me an answer. Nothing came.

"I'll give you some time to think it through and put matters in order. Time to let anybody know that needs to know. We don't need to make any decisions for the next hour."

An hour? That was all I had left to play God and dictate someone's fate? Was it a blessing to know he was in his last stages, and there would be no further carrot of hope dangled? I don't know. It didn't feel like a blessing in that moment.

I rang my brothers. The eldest would be over straight from work that evening, the other was too distraught to face him and wanted to hold onto the positive memory he held of him.

Deep breaths again. Ok. Let's do this. I consent. Let him go.

*

I walked back into my dad's room, held his cold withered hand, stroked his head, kissed him repeatedly, asked him if there was anything I could do to make him more comfortable and played music from his youthful years. It was a tip I'd been given by a friend for when people enter confusion, to bring them back to a time of comfort. It didn't help my dad. He was happier watching the TV, oblivious to me being there other than periodically squeezing my hand in return when I held it and asking on loop when he could go home. Soon, Dad. Soon.

I had to leave him to return to my own family. I wasn't there in his final moments; my brother was. Dad had woken very briefly, looked at my brother and said "I'm glad you're here" before his heart stopped beating, and he was finally pain-free at rest.

I returned the next morning to a lifeless body, the body I had nurtured the day before, the body that was previously warm, breathing and grasping my hand.

It wasn't real. He was still breathing I was sure of it. Someone had to check there was definitely no pulse. I couldn't possibly leave him there all alone. It was the last time I would see his body and I couldn't walk away.

An impulse ran through my mind. I had to take a photo. I had to take him with me.

Grief has a crazy way of making you do things that to a rational mind would seem absurd, but at that moment it made complete sense. It was all I had left. I took the photo on my phone, kissed his head and breathed in his essence.

As I walked to my car, I asked him to make me a promise in my head. That any time he wanted me to know he was watching over me, to appear as a squirrel. He had always loved Bob Ross and painting in a similar style, so it seemed the most apt thing to wish for.

Within a minute of thinking it, a squirrel ran across the grass. Two other squirrels appeared on my Facebook newsfeed within the next few hours and I felt at peace. Coincidence or not, it was a comfort. I looked at the photo later that night, said goodbye and deleted it. His body may be empty, but his spirit was with me.

His bristly moustache brushing my face, still a clear vision in my mind. What I would do to feel that in reality and smell his tobacco scent.

*

It would change my perspective on life completely. I wasn't going to live a life of waiting for happiness to happen. I had to shape my happiness.

We had moved again to a house in a better area. Our daughter was in a school that she felt happier in. My health was a lot better. Our finances were less strained. Yet those hairline fractures in the ice were now canyons within our marriage.

My decision to leave was the hardest decision I've ever faced.

It wasn't only my life that this would affect. It was the lives of my children and everyone else around them.

What if I wasn't enough for them? What if they grew up to hate me for making that choice? What if I regretted it myself? What if I stayed until they were teenagers and they lived in a house of resentment, walking on eggshells and never seeing deep connected love?

In the stillness, I knew what I had to do. We would have to hunker down and gather all our resources, but we were going to survive this hurricane.

Christmas wreaths upon the doors as reminders of life's thorns and the blood we shed, bold in their beauty. I would be facing many thorns and battling on wounded, but I would come out the other side just as bold.

Auld Lang Syne

We had never replaced the time we'd spent together dancing with anything else, and once our children were here, they were my new obsession. Sean was pushed aside. They were reliant on me, and he had to take the back seat now. Right from conception, my body became my children's. They were dependent on me for food in the early months, and I was happy that my body finally had a purpose, other than being a shell for someone else's sexual gratification.

There was no compromise in our conversations, no negotiation or debate. They became a playing field for point scoring and stabs of resentment. We no longer had each other's best interest at heart. We didn't show compassion or love for one another. We were too lost in exhaustion, stress, disconnection and loneliness.

We spoke about calling it quits several times. Apologised to each other, said we'd make more effort, and then pushed on hoping things would be different, which they often were, for a short while at least.

When we worked together, we were a good team. We ran our businesses together, us against the world. Until it wasn't anymore, and it was us against us.

*

The verbal attacks started subtly, but soon escalated into bitter stings of reactive venom.

Getting out of the house was not going to be an easy task. I had met a male friend at dancing who I was chatting to openly about life, unhappy marriage and how grief puts things into perspective, reminding us how short a time we have here. It was a huge blow to Sean's ego.

"You should be talking to me about everything, not him! You should be more committed to our marriage and we should have stuck with the couples' counselling." He stood so close to me that I could smell the nicotine on his clothes, with an accent of yesterday's stale alcohol on his breath.

I stepped back but could still feel his hand grasping my arm, partly in desperation, partly in anger.

"It's no good, Sean, we're going around in circles and neither of us is happy. We haven't been happy for years." I snatched myself away further.

"You're giving up because you've found something better. You're weak and you'll regret it because you'll never be happy. You're just going to go from one guy to another!" He was snarling like an injured animal now. Harsh and reactionary. Eyes glazed and stinging.

Attacking me with my own words of vulnerability and worries. He knew how I had sought love in others and how relationship after relationship had broken down because I couldn't fulfil the roles needed to sustain them. He knew how I hated feeling weak after spending so many years ill and fractured.

"Good luck to you, and good luck to him! I'm going to work." He stormed out, slamming the door and leaving a haze of disgust behind him.

Sean felt convinced that I was having an affair, and life became a rollercoaster of him begging me to change my mind, then causing me to break down in tears. It was emotionally abusive. I didn't blame him. I had destroyed his world as he knew it. To him, I had found a better model and was bailing out. To me, I was completely at the end of what I could give to our relationship, and I'd already put my life on hold for too long.

*

James had been in touch. His marriage had broken down with Sophie too. She had pulled a similar stunt with him by harming herself, then calling the police and blaming James. So, he finally believed my truth about *that fateful holiday.*

It was a strange feeling meeting up and talking about old times. It was a reminder of just how far I had come and how ambitious to live my life to the full I had once been.

I was determined not to lose sight of that and submit to defeat.

Things could never go back to how they once were between us. We were both different people now with our own responsibilities. He had a son, and I had my family. We couldn't spend nights going to the cinema or disappearing off for a week in the sun. We had grown up and laid down foundations in different woodlands, distant trees with our initials carved in each other's bark.

I started to really look at where I was in my life.

Daily diary entries would detail how low I was in the last three years of my marriage. On reflection, I'm sure there was postnatal depression that had been undiagnosed, but regardless there were issues that couldn't be ignored forever.

I'm walking through treacle, exhausted and torn by everyone's needs.

How can I make myself a priority when other people have expectations on me constantly? My time and energy are pushed to capacity. My ME has kicked off again, and I feel drained and depleted.

*

I'm so lost and lonely. My anxiety levels are through the roof and no-one is listening to me. I feel irritated by every small thing. The clocks have gone back, and it just means I get an extra hour of struggle to go through.

There's no communication with Sean anymore. I'm shouting at the kids for no reason, and the arguments are becoming a daily occurrence. I don't even know what we are arguing about. I wish I could shake off the negativity and not be so reactive, but I'm oblivious to how.

*

Any sparks of joy I ever felt have been long forgotten in the trudge of all this. I always end up right back to square one, bending for an easy life, knowing that there's really no such thing as an easy life.

My sense of guilt, anxiety and frustration are overwhelming whenever I think about my own needs. There's no point even going there. Each morning I wake up and say things are going to be different, and yet every day it ends up the same. Going to bed early to sleep is my only respite.

*

We're living like strangers under the same roof. Why am I even here? I'm an outsider in my own body. My head is cloudy, and my dreams vivid. I'm trying to get through one day at a time. Watching life happen but not actively participating in it.

I want to slap myself to wake up. I'm playing internal games of tug of war. Angry for not being able to just 'snap out of it', sad about my reactions towards the kids, then moving across to a sense of calm that it is ok to be still and not have all the answers, and a sense of brushing this all off and continuing to move forward as best I can.

*

Reading through the penned entries as I sat alone in the bedroom, I felt like an intruder in my own life. I was looking for clues and answers to piece together the puzzle of how numb I felt, and where I should go from there. Reading the words made me realise how much I focused on keeping someone else happy and how I neglected my own happiness as a result.

I had lost myself in the process of trying to live for others and playing the part of dutiful wife. I had stopped dancing, drawing, learning, laughing and loving. I had fought to hold everything together under volcanic pressure. If I was weak, there was no one else to take the reins and run things. I was completely exhausted with the process of being strong.

I wouldn't be able to look my children in their eyes when they were older and tell them to strive for their dreams if I had been too scared to do the same. I didn't want to demonstrate to my daughter that a healthy relationship looked like what she was witnessing with her parents. The anger, resentment, alternating who would play the victim or completely ignoring each other for days on end.

I didn't want to perpetuate the truth that abuse is something we must accept, that we need to be obedient and amiable and put up with men's behaviour regardless of how disempowering it feels.

At some point, I had to bite the bullet and leave, rather than just thinking about it. I had to take steps forward and define my boundaries. I was a mother, and all eyes were on me.

*

I never got married to get divorced. I got married because I was in love, and I had felt completely content with the person I was with. We danced together, went on crusades together and life felt like it made sense. Do I feel deep grief about the dreams I'd lost? Yes. But did I know when I had given my everything and it was time to walk away? Most certainly.

The role of dutiful wife wasn't going to fulfil my sense of self-worth any more than the roles of people pleaser/good little girl/best friend/long distance lover/rescuer/subservient/explorer or travelling romantic.

My worth had to come from me. From my own liberation and freedom. From the multi-faceted, multi-charactered, perfectly imperfect versions of me, coming together as one big collective Su.

*

I could no longer be with someone that I couldn't communicate with or relate to. It was affecting our daughter and that was a line that I had never wanted to be crossed.

"Please stop talking to each other with angry voices. It scares me." Her hands were covering her ears, and the wave of shame ran through my body like acid.

She hadn't been sleeping great, waking up with nightmares and complaining of stomach cramps. It was a clear sign to me that she was struggling to understand our difficulties and reacting with symptoms of anxiety. I couldn't let that happen. Anxiety ran through my veins far too easily, and it wasn't a trait I wanted to pass down.

*

We were all living in a strange limbo state. A family of robotic routines, that were the last thing that made sense, but the only things that held the house together. I was still making meals, washing and organising, but the love was stripped away from the acts like maple bark. I was no longer sharing a bed with Sean, and we were no longer sharing a connection.

I cried more than I had in my whole life collectively in those last few months of living together. I felt trapped in a situation that was unbearable and was questioning myself constantly. It was an alien existence and I didn't know what to expect from one day to the next.

*

"I've just had a phone call from Sean. He said you were spending time with a paedophile now! He's being completely irrational again. Are you ok?"

My mum had witnessed me breaking down, not knowing what to do, many a time. Here I was, back in her cream cosy sanctuary of a front room, waiting for a cup of tea and catching my breath.

"You can't keep picking up the pieces for him my love. He is obviously broken, and you are worn down. He isn't going to change."

She had seen me and Sean together on holidays, she had seen him sit round the pool while I chased around after our daughter exhausted, she had seen us battle over our differences, so she knew that things had been strained for many years, but that it had become much more unsettled and erratic lately.

She sighed and handed me the warm mug of respite. Winnie the Pooh printed on the side. I was still her baby girl.

She went on "I don't even know where he's got this latest delusion from? I've asked him not to ring us anymore. You're my daughter and he has his own family for support."

"I know Mum. I'm not even dating anyone. He's desperate for someone to give him answers that give him something to blame. He's been messaging several friends trying to find out where I am and what I'm up to, but there's nothing for him to discover."

"Just be careful, my love. Ring that phone number your friend gave you for the family safety unit and see if they have any advice? I'm worried about you and the kids."

We had already fled to my sister in laws the weekend before for the night because the arguments were mentally exhausting. I never feared him hitting me, despite him throwing things around the room when he was angry. But the constant interrogation and tracking of my movements was completely draining.

"I will, Mum. It will all be ok."

Sean had openly admitted to going through my things and reading my diary. He had refused me use of the joint car, so I was getting taxis or picked up by friends to go anywhere I needed to. It had almost become normal just plodding on.

The next discovery would be the one that made me realise I needed to do something, and plodding would not suffice.

*

I got home to an empty house. I had been sleeping on our son's floor for weeks, so had barely gone into our bedroom other than to get some fresh clothes. I needed a warmer jumper, and went to grab one from my old cupboards, only to be faced with a shrine of photos of our wedding day, photos of the kids, jewellery, gifts we'd exchanged and a letter.

To Su,

My wife and the mother of our children.

I can still be the man that you want to spend the rest of your life with.

I'm sorry if I've not been the best husband to you. I've made mistakes and learnt from them.

You mean everything to me, and I love you and miss you so much.

Hope for a future!

Love Sean

The tears poured out of my eyes without reprieve. This was the same man who earlier that morning had told me he hated everything about me, that I had ruined his life, that he wished he'd never met me and if I was going to my mum's I should stay there and die.

I wanted to believe the words of the letter, but I had heard them so many times before. This time I couldn't go back.

I rang the family safety unit and completed a risk assessment. I had never even considered my situation to be that big a deal, but the woman on the phone told me otherwise.

"From the questions you've answered, you are considered high risk within the domestic violence categories."

"But he's never hit me?"

"No, but he has manipulated and emotionally abused you. We can arrange for a space in a refuge for you and the kids to go tonight. Can you pack bags ready? I will give you all the details you need. Do you have a pen and somewhere safe you can write things down?"

Brain went into a panic. *A refuge? Where the kids would only have one teddy and a bag of clothes. Surely they'd been through enough already?*

Heart was racing around my chest like a thunderstorm in a tornado.

Don't forget to breathe. Inhale for four, hold for two, exhale for six.

My shoulders fell slowly.

"Can I try and get him out of the house first? I'm worried about uprooting the kids and I think I can convince him to go if he knows he might never see the kids again if he doesn't." This would be my toughest stand off to date, but the stakes were high, and I needed to at least attempt to keep my cubs in their den.

"Of course. You know your situation better than anyone. Just give us a ring back by 6pm so we can make any arrangements if needed. If you are concerned about yours or the kid's safety at any point ring 999 and in the meantime contact someone you trust to let them know what's going on."

I hung up the phone in a daze. This wouldn't be the reaction Sean was expecting with his love note.

*

The kids were in afterschool club. I had to do this before they came home.

The click of the front door pounded in my stomach and sent shock waves throughout my whole body.

I walked down the stairs trying to remain calm and remember to breathe. I was two-foot-tall facing the mountain of Sean in front of me. His athletic build wasn't domineering, but his presence preceded him with the potent 'Millions' aftershave entering the room before him. The smell that I used to inhale with such pleasure, now a reminder of the past and how drastically things had changed. His hair seeming much greyer now, his wrinkles much deeper. Had we both aged suddenly in the grief of our demise?

"We can't do this anymore, Sean. You need to go," I stated it quickly, rehearsed and cutting, somehow managing to keep my voice steady.

"What are you talking about? I'm not going anywhere. This is your doing, and you can go if you want to destroy a family for a guy you've just met." He leaned against the wall, his mouth set in a firm line, his tone cold.

"I've spoken to the family safety unit and we have a place in a refuge waiting for us tonight." I watched his expression change, his eyes wide with outrage. "If you don't leave by six, then you won't know where we are, or be able to see the kids indefinitely."

"A refuge? What the hell? I've never even touched you. You've gone mad! I'd never hurt my kids." He moved towards me, his arms held out like he was harmless and just wanted to reason with me. I knew better.

My heart was beating out of my chest.

Memories of days being screamed at by partners, of being slapped, of being dragged around by my hair, of having my hand crushed when I tried to phone the police, of being crushed under the weight of a lead body wanting pleasure and being told I was nothing, all jerked to the forefront of my mind. No, Sean had never touched me with his fists in the same way, but he could make me feel just as worthless and broken.

I took a step away from him. "You have to go." "I can't believe you're doing this!" His face was a crippling blend of rage, devastation and disbelief. It took a strength that I didn't even know I had to stand so coldly in front of him, firm in my decision. Crumbling inside and wanting to make it all go back to how it once was. Gliding across the dancefloor with grace and ease.

The fear in every inch of me quivered beneath the surface but was cleverly masked by the thick bark above. He knew I was serious and that there was no turning back now.

It was brutal that it had to get to that point. The only man I truly ever loved was being forced into a corner simply because we were so filled with insecurity and hate, that we couldn't talk anymore.

*

His dad came to collect him, all anger directed at me. "Where's my son?"

I could see where Sean had got his bulldog grit from now.

Sean trundled past me, silent but ominous and laden down with a suitcase. He bundled the life he had gathered up, into the boot of his dad's car. The solemn death of our marriage in one grey coffin of a bag. No elegy to be sung here. Just the sound of the car driving off and the end of an era.

I picked the kids up and told them that Daddy would be staying with Nannie and Grandad for a while. We had dinner, and the evening continued with a formal but silent edge.

After weeks on the floor, I was able to sleep in our marital bed again. It was the most surreal feeling. It wasn't a win for me. None of it was. This wasn't a game of winners. This was survival of a family unit, under circumstances that were never a desirable conclusion.

I had already cried a deluge of agony, but I would cry so much more. This is what my life had come to. I had the children that had given me a reason to fight for life, but I'd lost my partner in the process. It felt like such cruelty.

The ceiling was my television. Staring into blank space for hours, hoping that some sort of clarity would come, that I would get a deep reassurance that I'd done the right thing. I was hoping for a sign from somewhere telling me everything would be ok.

There was no reassurance. There was no sign. There was just emptiness waiting to be filled, by what I didn't quite know.

Yesterday's Gone By

Should we forget our lovers knot and how our roots entwined?
Should we forget the growth we shared, and yesterday's gone by?

For old times' sake my love, for days gone by.
We'll take a breath of winter air, for yesterday's gone by.

We shared the woods with branches strong and seedlings under foot
But faced just one too many storms to batter and uproot.

We tried our best to weather life and hold our blossom strong.
But in the end the wind blew wild and snatched our flowers along.

For old times' sake my love, for days gone by.
We'll take a breath of winter air for yesterday's gone by.

And surely you will bloom again, and surely so will I.
And we'll take a breath of winter air for yesterday's gone by.

My branches still reach out to yours and hope yours reach for mine.
To shelter those we cherish most, for yesterday's gone by.

For old times' sake my love, for days gone by.
We'll take a breath of winter air, for yesterday's gone by.
For old times' sake my love, for days gone by.
We'll take a breath of winter air, for yesterday's gone by.

It would be a long time before those breaths of winter air would be shared for the sake of days gone by, and for the sake of our saplings needing protection. For now, my branches would have to battle off the storms alone.

Promising Resolutions

It took another two months for me to find and secure a new house local to where we were. A sanctuary to escape from the chaos that had been before. Something that was solely mine and the kids.

I hadn't wanted to uproot them too much. This had to be somewhere we could move to and settle as a new family of three for a significant amount of time.

*

It had been a battle trying to find somewhere. I was a single mum, partly on benefits, with a small self-employed income and two children under seven. I wasn't an appealing prospect.

On the day of moving my new landlord turned up at our old property, as the washing machine was being loaded onto the van with the last few bits.

"I'm afraid there's a problem." His face was as white as his hair. "I don't think you can move in, because you lied to us."

A wrecking ball to the chest smashed without warning.

"Excuse me?" What on earth was he talking about?

"You didn't tell us you had kids and we don't want them at the property."

Was I in a parallel universe here? Was Jeremy Beadle about to jump out and shout 'you've been framed!'?

Deep breaths. Deep breaths.

"I told you I had a daughter and we spoke about how she would love the garden. I've never kept it a secret that I have kids. I never would. They are my world."

My voice was shaking and the fear in my mouth tasted like a crushing release. My head spun around like a waltzer at high speed.

"The house is my wife's pride and joy and we had wanted a young professional to move in. I'm not sure you're suitable, erm, I'm not sure it's suitable for you."

The words had already been said. He had cast judgement on me for the situation I had found myself in.

"I'll have to speak to the agents and get back to you." He was pale with a side note of fluster, but seemed to be suppressing it well, some attempt of keeping things business like maybe. It felt like he was the messenger rather than the leader.

He walked off, mobile pressed to his ear as if he had just delivered the most everyday news.

The floor beneath my feet had capsized. I was stood in a deep ravine, my belongings loaded onto a van, the hope I had fought for of being in a safe home that was mine, sat on a vast mountain in front of me. Out of reach.

*

I would have to stay where I was, knowing that Sean could enter at will with his keys anytime he wanted. He had been to the house a couple of times already while I was out, collected more of his stuff and left hints of his life without me. Cigarette butts in the sink, packets of condoms at the top of the boxes he didn't have room in the car for, energy drinks cans. A rebellious teenager who could live how he chose to now, without a nagging wife to pass comment.

There was little I could do unless I got the police involved. His name was on the tenancy and I had no right to change the locks. There had been enough drama already so I put up with it, clinging to the belief I would be out of there soon.

Now I was being told that I might have to stay trapped a while longer? Not without a fight!

*

The next hour was a swirling snowstorm of crying and pleading phone calls to the estate agent, hearing that I should move into the new house regardless, that the landlord had no choice in the matter, that the contracts had been signed and there had been no clause stating that children weren't allowed, so he had no legal rights to stop things going ahead.

I was to empty my belongings into a house that I wasn't welcome in, then have the landlord come around and apologise for the upset.

Maybe I had imagined the whole scene, it had been so surreal and traumatic.

I prayed it wasn't an omen for things to come. For once I didn't want to believe in signs. I needed some good fortune this time.

*

Thankfully we settled quickly. This was our new normal, our new life, our new world. None of it was easy, but all of it was worth it.

This was a stable and secure environment for my children grow and thrive.

We could be still for a while now. Strong in our roots with promising times ahead.

We had weathered the storm and soon it would be spring again.

Standing Tall Again

There were so many skills to learn, that I would cry from the depths of my soul, each tear coming from deeper within, releasing the pain from my core and leaving me exhausted and spent.

I cried for the young girl bullied at school, the lost teenager, the anxious young woman trapped in abusive relationships and the mother lacking self-belief. I cried for the dreams I missed out on, the things I never said to those passed and the woman who was yet to follow and reflect on her life with a sense of pride.

Those following months I would shout lots. I would hug lots, and I would smile lots, but I could no longer run away.

This was all on me to work through and figure out. These children needed me more than ever before and I wasn't about to let them down.

*

Separation is unbelievably life-changing and challenging. It can feel overwhelming and isolating, but it was through my separation that I found my voice and started to open up about some of the struggles I had faced throughout my life.

It was these reflections that gave me the motivation to write blogs, for my words to help another person reach out or realise that they are normal for finding some days so difficult, so I felt compelled to write. About everything.

I wondered if I was enough on my own, constantly. I tried not to overcompensate and be both parents in one but couldn't help but push myself harder because the responsibility lay on my shoulders alone.

You were the one who made the choice to leave, so now it's up to you to lie in the bed you've made. Oh brain, I can't say I've missed you.

*

I faced rebuilding a whole new life, with a significant piece missing in the puzzle. The previous picture had never quite fit together properly, yet it still left me feeling lost in an abyss of unknowns about what that new life even looks like.

It became a juggling act of trying to create a sense of normality and stability within a whole new family dynamic, whilst also trying to maintain healthy relationships with what were now 'ex' family members, so that things didn't feel 'too different' or unsettling.

Blending lives that were now on such independent courses and directions was an art I was yet to master.

I felt selfish, like a failure, like I gave up too easily, like I didn't deserve love or happiness like I'd damaged my children in some way, like I was open to abuse and criticism because it was largely my decision to be here.

I'd forgotten what led me to that choice point, how I'd cried more times than I could count, felt disconnected, empty and alone. How I was filled with resentment and anger and I'd lost sight of what was truly important.

*

I had to remind myself that modelling to your children that a healthy relationship is run on arguments and upset, not love and resolution would not be 'staying together for their sake'. I also had to remember about teaching them how to have healthy relationships with themselves.

People would say things like: "you're so strong" or "you're brave for leaving", but I didn't feel either. I didn't leave a brutal tyrant. I left a toxic situation that developed because of two people unable to communicate effectively, and that was as much my responsibility as anyone else's.

*

So how do you start again when the world as you knew it has been turned upside down?

One day at a time, with the support of amazing friends and family, and by paying attention to your wins, no matter how small – the kid's laughter, doing things you never thought were possible and making it through the day alive.

By writing your story and listening to other's stories, by being grateful for the lessons learned and teaching your children that life can be messy, but you will always find a way through. It's not a smooth or easy ride, but you aren't alone.

See yourself in all your amazing beauty, with the leaves of doubt and struggle shed. A weathered but strong tree filled with characteristics shaped by experience.

All the parts I have played in my life have taught me things. Some have taught me about things I wouldn't return to, but some have brought out qualities in me that I couldn't imagine existed.

There would be honesty in our house. There would be no secrets and there would be communication. Questions would be answered as best as they could be. Apologies would be given when things got too much for any of us.

We would learn that it's not about being perfect. Life isn't perfect. It's a jumble of experience and emotions that are up and down, but we make the most of the ups and can ride through the downs.

I am grateful for my children. They have taught me more about what's important in life than any other experience. They are my root system. They nourish me with their wisdom, inquisitive nature and unconditional love and I shelter them with my branches. I write this book for them. To prove that no matter what mistakes you make, what experiences you must go through, what difficulties you face, you can come out standing tall and strong. The tree–filled with unique beauty in every season.

The maturing woman contemplating her seasons so far. Of the budding child, the fiery teenager, the younger woman shedding layers and the winter of motherhood beginning. Each season with its own lessons and characteristics. All moving forward at different rates with different intensity. All needed. All important. All interconnected in a symphony with beautiful, solemn, upbeat, slow music created. The chorus of the trees. The tree that is me.

The Second Spring

So here I am four decades later. A lone parent. A women's empowerment and resilience coach. A writer. An honest and loyal friend. A fragile, imperfect, yet strong woman with a story to tell and a journey to share.

I enter now into my second spring. The 'midlife crisis'. The rebirth after knowing all that you know, that you wish you knew years ago.

Ready to face the challenges of what the next decade or four bring. Ready to embrace the cycles of my seasons.

Ready to honour the learning that is yet to come and hoping I've inspired others to do the same.

I now know when I set my mind to something, I can create it.

I was determined to fight anorexia-bulimia, and I did.

I was determined to build my own business, and I did.

I was determined to be able to speak in public, and I did.

I was determined to write a book, and I have.

I was determined to build a group of supportive women, and I have.

I was determined to let go of unhealthy relationships and habits, and I have.

My next goals are to continue be a good role model for my children, to inspire thousands of women and men to step into their power and to continue to grow and evolve constantly.

I welcome in the second spring of fresh opportunity, adventure and learning. I'm no longer that shy, fearful child of my first spring. My branches are stronger now and formed with beautiful imperfections. I am unashamed of my presence, because I know my story needs sharing. It may not be well-received by all who read it, but it has a space to be told and I'm grateful for that.

I know that others have the same determined spirit inside them and often it just needs some light shining on it in order to grow. I hope to bring some of that light, a glimmer that things can be different and that challenges can be overcome.

You are possibly reading this because you want to see a fresh perspective, and I know that you can make changes. I am not here to save anyone or give them models to live by. I am simply here to share a journey and the insight I gained personally. Take the parts that make sense to you and create your own insight.

You are destined to be a mighty oak.

*

How do you let go of addiction?

You don't, completely. You learn to accept it as part of you and minimise your need for it in your life by filling the gap with things that serve you and heal you, instead of hurting you.

I don't pretend that I'll never want to skip a meal when I'm stressed, binge when there's too much temptation around, or purge if I'm in discomfort. But if it ever does happen, I will brush myself off, remind myself how my kids need me strong, and start fresh as soon as I'm able to.

Beating ourselves up for relapses is never beneficial. It was low self-worth that kept the destructive cycles going for so long and what I have strived to let go of.

*

Will I ever fall in love again?

I don't know, but I know any future relationships will be entered with open communication right from the start. That I will acknowledge what is my experience, my scars and my suffering so that I don't project those struggles onto a partner.

I will own my challenges, talk about them, and let go of the need for answers or validation, and I will learn to truly listen in return, keeping my heart as open as I can.

It is when we have expectations, and fail to listen, that resentment builds up and takes over. I am not willing to let that happen easily again.

I will continue to develop my skills in patience, gratitude, and a sense of humour. All of which have a very strong place within a relationship. It's important to be able to learn and plan together, laugh together, cry together and make time for each other so that you both feel valued.

I no longer expect things to run smoothly all the time, I know that there will be highs and lows, but I also know that I can trust my instincts more and when things feel disconnected, that I will be able to face them.

I have known the crippling pain of long-term loneliness and the longing for understanding. I have withdrawn from people as a result and I have rejected love.

I know that loneliness comes from a feeling that no-one truly knows you or accepts you as you are, but I also know that a sense of acceptance and understanding comes from the self-first. Once you master that, then you no longer need to seek it in another, and relationships become more about sharing a journey than making each other whole.

You are already whole.

*

I've come to realise that humans sometimes require reaching the depths of despair and the lowest point possible, to find the fighting spirit that we have within.

We become complacent so easily when life manages to somehow tick along. It's only when we have lost all our fingers, that we realise how much we needed our hands. I aim to stop people needing to suffer to realise their importance.

To see that we don't need to go through such adversity to grow, that every little experience we go through shapes us and creates a unique story that has a place on this earth.

I invite you to embrace the seasons of your own life and know that each has their place.

Springs Lessons of Creativity and Choice

That immature child had learned a lot already.
Faced with rejection and loneliness she had retreated inwards and created a fantasy reality that no-one could judge or take away from her.
She had developed skills that would see her through every season, the start of a root system forming and giving her the strength to continue.

The Power of Creativity

Creativity gives us a sense of potential when we're in a state of helplessness and allows us to see things from a different perspective.

It gives us time to stop daydreaming and start life dreaming.

As we grow up life seems to become about responsibility and control.

The lands of adventure can lay dormant for a long while.

Revisit those lands. Dream again.

It is important to be grounded in the here and now, to get a lot of practical things done during our day, but we also need the time and space to dream and create.

Creativity flow calms our mind, boosts our energy levels, and provides clarity about what we would want our life to look like if we had no restrictions of fear/financial stress/skill-set or geographical location.

When we permit ourselves to life dream and start to believe that we are worthy of having that life, it initiates a shift in our brain that allows us to be more open to opportunities that come our way.

When we restrict our ideas and creativity, those same opportunities will come our way but will be brushed off as pipe dreams. We won't believe ourselves capable of really having them, or they seem so far out of reach we wouldn't know where to begin to accept them as truths.

Allowing more creativity into your life can start as small as you like. Small steps can lead to big leaps over time.

Think about what made you smile when you were that young child dreaming the days away.

What do you get so lost in that your sense of time gets forgotten about?

What lifts you up and you couldn't imagine living life without?

These are the keys to unlocking your energy, your inspiration, your motivation and keep you going in those times of monotony, struggle and boredom.

Acknowledge those things and simply do more of them every day.

Whether it's dancing, drawing, writing, singing, playing music, painting, yoga or sky diving, there will be an activity that gets you into a state of flow.

A place where you feel at home in yourself. A place where you can think about your life and know what you would like to change. A place that acts as a base for you to springboard from. A place that nourishes you, fills you with life force energy and allows you to expand and grow.

We all have our unique skills. We all have our unique beliefs. We all have our unique dreams. We all contain our own magic. Whatever lights your soul. Do much more of that.

Letting Gratitude Blossom

Returning to the innocence of childhood and seeing life through immature eyes brings us back to a sense of gratitude. It allows us to remember how precious life is and gives us the power to let go of self-judgement.

You may have come across the exercise of being your own best friend and reflecting on where you currently are with kindness, but I want to take that a step further and reflect on where you are through a child's eyes, therefore adding in a frame of awe and wonder

Instead of looking at yourself through eyes of judgement, notice every detail as if you were drawing a person for the first time. Going from the stick figures of a circle with two legs to the beautiful artwork that you are. Every blemish, every wrinkle, every curve, every bump. They are all uniquely you.

Start to see your attributes and qualities above your imperfections and witness the intricacy of what has made you who you are today. Humans are genuinely incredible. We are faced with such adversities, yet continue to grow, to move, to learn and to form relationships, sometimes without even acknowledging how huge a task that has been.

Children won't describe people as 'fat', 'ugly' or 'unworthy' until they are taught the words. Even then, they don't have a sense of meaning to them. It is us that goes on to give them meaning and us that gives that meaning weight in our lives.

Know that you have a choice to use new words, and to give old words new meaning.

Creatively Crying

Don't be afraid to let the tears fall. Your vulnerability is your power. There is a release in those tears. They have held you prisoner to your brave face and sometimes they need to just cascade.

As babies, our natural form of communication is through tears. It is seen as the sign of a healthy baby when the midwives hear that first cry, because it indicates that the child's lungs are strong.

Somewhere along the line, we are taught that those tears are a sign of weakness and should be filled with a sense of embarrassment and shame, when they are actually our strength.

When we acknowledge the sadness for what it is, we release the stored trauma, and we embrace our vulnerability, creating space for magic and clarity.

We need to start looking closer at what is causing those droplets to form in the creases of our eyes and what they are trying to tell us.

How can we use that knowledge to create change?

Crying should be accepted as being as normal as laughter when we have seen something funny. Tears of sadness are just the flip side to the coin, and they are just as necessary for a balanced life.

What beliefs do you currently have about crying?

If you went back to your younger self at a point of upset and gave them a reassuring hug, how would that feel

What triggers you to feel upset?

Spend time journaling your answers.

Look at your beliefs and see if they still feel true to you.

Are they useful beliefs to hold?

Do they keep you safe, or could you start to let them go and form new ones?

Creative Happiness

Most of us have been nicely trained since childhood in the art of not wanting for more. Being thankful for what we have because there are so many others without. Being humble and kind or giving selflessly to others with a sense of pride. But we are also bombarded with messages about what we 'should have' in our lives to feel successful and happy.

How often do we stop to ask ourselves what really would make us feel successful and happy? What would add value to our microcosm?

This exercise is not about being greedy, ungrateful or neglecting others' needs. It is about realising that the more you give to you, then the more energy you have for others. It is about seeing that the more you seek out what is truly important to you, the more aligned you will become to your genuine happiness.

Let me put this into context – how energised do you feel when something goes right for you? You got the job you've always wanted; you got the house you dreamed of, your kids got into the nicest school, your work has had an amazing review, you got the all-clear on a health scare. You are on cloud nine, and most people are full of excitement to share that with others.

When we're happy our bodies produce serotonin, dopamine, oxytocin and opiates. Strive for what makes you feel fulfilled, and you will fill up on these feel-good hormones.

When I ask what is missing in your life right now, this isn't about the latest BMW series, to be a size eight or Brad Pitt to knock on your door tomorrow (although dream for any of those if you wish).

This is about wanting a greater sense of purpose, more creativity, more adventure, more time for travel, more love, to be physically fitter, to be able to say no guilt-free, to have more energy, or all the above.

You may be in a place where you feel 'I am not enough' or 'I don't deserve what I want', but just by visualising change you can reach a point of 'I've had enough' of things the way they currently are, and it can drive you to take action. It doesn't have to be resolutions at New Year or the death of a loved one that spurs you on. Where you put your attention is where it goes.

We get to choose.

Start to visualise your life as a storyboard.

Who would surround you?

What sort of work would you be doing?

What would your daily life look like?

What things would light up the picture and make it more vibrant and desirable?

Are you living in the area you currently live in?

What foods are you eating?

What clothes are you wearing?

The clearer you can make your storyboard life, the more your brain connects with that image and begins to open up to the possibility of it happening.

This isn't magic. Manifestation is simply allowing your mind to focus on possibility and then allowing that possibility to happen. Mindset is the key to it all. When you can accept abundance as your new story and see the value in having money to give more of yourself to the world with less restriction, then receiving it will have greater value and you will spend it a lot more wisely.

The same is true for any aspirations. When we see value in ourselves, then the life we want to create has value far greater than any advertising campaign can throw at us.

We begin to value our bodies, so we want to feed it nutritious foods and have movement in our days. We begin to value our time, so we want to make the most of every hour instead of spending it in an unfulfilling job. We begin to value our friendships, so we create time to build upon them. This isn't about leaving your stable job and moving to Bali. Look at where you would truly love to be in five years and make small changes to get there. Look honestly at your life and what isn't working or giving you self-worth. You are in the driver's seat and you hold the power to change.

Creative Communication

We have become such an insular and disconnected society, fearful of expressing opinions and feelings, and we often prevent others from knowing who we truly are.

We try so desperately to avoid the pain that may come as a result of our honesty, whether that is rejection or judgement, that we lose our childlike ability to be an open book. To cry when we're upset, to laugh, to play, to create, to give out hugs randomly, to hope, to dream.

We have built up walls around ourselves to protect our hearts from pain, but this prevents us from knowing each other on a deeper level.

There is a simple, yet powerful exercise to develop the skill of open communication and start the butterfly effect for others to do the same.

Send a message to someone in your life telling them you are thinking of them and that you want to share how you see them. This can be their qualities, their strengths, their creativity, their kindness, their passions or something they have taught you. You may also want to gift them with something that they might need to hear, such as the ability to feel proud of their achievements.

An example would be I see you... (insert their name here) as a strong, inspiring and caring person, who has taught me about resilience and who I gift with the ability of self-love.

Just the process of sending someone an acknowledgement of your appreciation for them in your life, allows dialogue to open up. They may never have been so compassionate towards themselves or may have had a completely different view of how others saw them. It permits them to be less critical of themselves, if only for that brief moment.

Without those open conversations, we miss out on those magical moments of real connection. We can spend our lives carrying guilt and pain about our perception of events, rather than a sense of peace knowing we have lived our lives without regret and told the people that matter how much we love them.

When we start to form those deeper relationships with others, the self-critic inside loses their grip on us and the battle with brain subsides. We can reflect on situations with open ears, and it allows us to do the same in return.

Building a tribe gives us strength that can't be easily wavered.

Choice

Whatever path you take, you will handle it.

There is no roadmap to life. We can have ideas laid out in front of us, but there are no instructions for the *right* ideas.

Whichever route you take, you will manage the outcome, and it's ok to change your route when it's headed somewhere you no longer want to go.

As a child, there's very little to think about or consider. Your decisions are limited to whether you want beans on toast or spaghetti Bolognese for dinner and you don't get caught up on which is the 'right' choice. It's a straight-forward problem because either way you know you will be fed.

As adults, we have greater freedom of choice, but also a greater sense of responsibility to choose correctly. We forget that ability to just go with the flow and make the most of whatever we decide without judgement. Suddenly those choices come with consequences and we often get torn between our head and heart.

We get given conflicting advice and start to ignore our instincts altogether. We lose trust in ourselves and trust in the people around us. We stay in our comfort zone, afraid to make any decisions out of fear of going down the wrong path.

How do you develop a greater sense of self-acceptance and courage?

By making the decisions and embracing the outcomes regardless of how they look.

In every outcome, there is something to gain. Whether that's a lesson about how you want to do something differently, a discovery that you can do even more, or the realisation that you need to start your plan from scratch. There will always be things to reflect upon and learn.

The first step is just making a choice. Any choice. Then acting upon that choice and observing what happens.

Commit to yourself. Start to build a relationship with yourself again. Know that whatever happens, you will handle it. You are filled with strength, power and excitement that is just waiting to be recognised and utilised. You are stronger than you currently believe and braver than you know.

Whatever decision you make, if it isn't to cause harm to another, it doesn't matter, it's all experience, and you will adapt to whatever you face. We are designed to survive. We have resilience and determination built into our wiring, and every challenge we face is part of our journey.

Embrace your instincts and what they are telling you, but remember that whatever path you take, you will handle it.

Summers Lessons of Self-Acceptance

That young teenager faced some tough experiences.
Physical abuse, sexual abuse, emotional abuse, illness.
Feeling lost in the woods She would have to accept some of her imperfections to grow any further, speak some of her truths out loud, embrace her shadows and learn the first steps towards self-love.

Facing the Past and Speaking Your Truth

What would it mean to lay your life bare for everyone to see?

Revealing all the darkest secrets, shames, guilts and regrets in their full glory without filter?

To be free of self-doubt and move to self-acceptance and self-love?

So many of us have stories that we swear we will take to our grave, but who are we protecting by doing so?

We forget that we are all here for human experience. We all hold those shadows that linger beside us like yesterday's perfume. Those raw truths that almost feel unbearable to even bring to the forefront of your mind.

We have buried them with stacks of pillows as silencers, and rationalised why those events happened, by sugar coating them with our own self-doubt.

Our mind accepts the abuse – because it wasn't their fault, their childhood was filled with abuse too and they had to express that pain somewhere.

We wear our humiliation and embarrassment like an internal straight jacket, using it to justify why our life has evolved the way it has – because we are flawed and deserve struggle.

Our remorse becomes a heavy weight upon our shoulders repressing our creativity and drive – because things could have been different, if only we had said no, tried harder, turned in a different direction.

We think that our whole world will cascade down around us when we speak these truths, that we will be locked away by men in white coats, laughed at or rejected. But we become lighter, liberated and wish we'd shouted them from the roof-tops years before. We give permission for the world that sees us, to be courageous and do the same.

There is a power in that vulnerability. That pure self-acceptance for everything you have lived and the opportunity to use that as fuel for what you do next.

When you speak your truth, things will change within you. Your sense of self-respect has room to grow and how you express yourself becomes easier. New and nourishing habits can be formed, as you remove the baggage that has held you back for so long.

You can begin to become the person you have always wanted to be and move forward one tiny step at a time.

We all have experiences in our lives that shape the course of the decisions we make from that point forward. They almost define who we are as a person and our identity within the world.

Some of these experiences can be very proud moments we've had, achievements we've made or people that we have loved, but some of these moments can be ones where our control and power has been taken away, and our understanding of how we go on to process those moments of discomfort and challenge.

Often when we are faced with those difficult situations, we revert inwards; we hold onto that guilt, fear, anger, upset or just plain confusion and that can fester within us, breeding self-doubt, self-hate and a lack of self-confidence. We make decisions based on how we feel about ourselves in this low state and that can go on to perpetuate the problem.

We believe we are worthless, and almost go on to prove the fact by the choices we make from that point forward. We go into self-destruct mode, negative bias, where everything is doomed.

Your heart is as strong as spider silk, woven with strands of experience.

You are a survivor. You have the resilience of a coiled spring and the determination of an ant carrying three times its own body weight. You have all the answers inside about what you need to do, you just need to allow the mental chatter to soften so you can hear clearly once more. You are as fragile as a bomb with more power inside than you can even comprehend.

As your glass armour shatters around you it leaves behind a thousand tiny gems reflecting to you your strength in prisms of light. Allow yourself to witness the pain, forgive yourself for not having all the answers right now, embrace the love of those around you that care, look up to the sun for energy and remember that like the ocean these waves will ebb and flow.

It isn't easy to face yourself, but there may well be someone who hears your voice inside themselves and is waiting to learn that they aren't alone. Your words can inspire more than you imagine, and in those words lies your unbreakable strength.

Look a bit deeper at the beliefs you have about yourself, challenge them, question where they have come from and start to at least listen to your truth, even if you can't speak it out loud. Your story is valid, and your story is real.

Living Your Truth

Living your truth to me means showing up, even when you are consumed with self-doubt, and pushing through that fear and anxiety.

It means doing the things you have held back from and living your life as if it means something, because guess what? It does!

No-one has your experience, your wisdom, your skills or your dreams in quite the same combination as you have, so use that to your advantage.

There is no such thing as perfection. No-one has it all sorted. People need to witness your journey because you have gifts to share in that learning and growth. Nobody is stopping you from living your truth, but you. So, what are you waiting for?

Opening up to self-care and doing work to tackle self-esteem, confidence and self-worth brings all sorts of magical moments, and the work has true value.

You will finally be able to look in the mirror and say to the person who looks back that they're ok. You will attract people who want to be there to lift you and cheer you on. You will see opportunity, where previously you just saw challenge, and life will feel richer.

Within that magic there lies an acceptance that the truth of your past has shaped who you are. Part of the work is witnessing the things that happened as merely experiences or lessons and forgiving yourself.

There is no special formula to erase your past, but you have the choice of how that shapes your future. You can use it as fuel to light your fire or you can allow it to eat away at you like cancer. You deserve more. You have gifts to share. You are loved and you have the power to step out of your comfort zone and live your truth.

Try writing your own bucket list. Start with the small things that challenge you and as you gain confidence you can try the bigger things.

The Battle with Self-Doubt

It’s a life’s battle challenging the thoughts that have been programmed into every cell and being. Events become distorted to prove that you can’t possibly change your life. Critical information is deleted from the equation and you generalise what the outcome will be. This is fundamentally how our brain works and how it makes sense of the world around us. Distortion, deletion or generalisation.

All of this can be overcome once you acknowledge that self-doubt is just part of the process, and you can remind yourself of why you wanted to make the changes in the first place. Self-doubt only happens when you are moving forward, so count it as a sign you are going in the right direction.

We need to appreciate that self-work never ends. We are constantly a work in progress and there will be times that we don’t feel on our game.

We read the books, attend the courses, do the journaling, forgive our past choices and hug the inner child, and yet we all still have days when the doubts creep in, and we are faced with anxiety that we know has no real substance, but start to question everything.

What if it’s our gut instinct telling us we're on the wrong path? Maybe the planets aren't aligned properly, and we just need to wait it out, or maybe we have finally realised we're not good enough/too old/not the right person for the job.

Or...

Maybe you've just pushed yourself out of your comfort zone more recently. You're growing, becoming more aware of how you're living your life and where you want to focus your energy, and a little bit of resistance and fear is creeping in.

Those times when the indecision sets in. When you feel overwhelmed and that you’ve taken on way more than you can handle. When you feel like life is simpler when you stay in the background, the observer, the lurker. Maybe it would be best to just stay there. Then there would be no worry or stress. Everything would be filled with rainbows and glitter there.

Except we know we can’t and don’t want to settle for a mediocre life of monotony and status quo. It’s pleasant for a short while, but most humans seek adventure and excitement. It stimulates our growth. We look for things that challenge us, even if we never sign up to doing them. We watch others living out our dreams and wish we could do the same, forgetting that we can.

We do have the ability to live out our dreams and it's not about living completely without anxiety or fear. It's about challenging yourself to push through it regardless and being honest about when you've been holding yourself back.

You will doubt and you will resist, but the world needs you exactly as you are, so stop hiding away from it.

The fact is, that we're all needed exactly as we are, and at some point, you just need to become friends with the self-doubt and ignore all its outdated advice.

Even before we've done all the self-work, yoga retreats, coaching courses or listened to every podcast on overcoming limiting beliefs we are needed.

That rawness, that vulnerability, that resilience and determination. That is what lights others up. That is what allows them to do the same and gives them permission to be just as raw and real. In a world filled with filters who doesn't want more real?

Self-Acceptance & Self-Love

Having the ability to start showing yourself the compassion we all deserve, and healing the trauma scars we have faced, is one of the greatest steps you can take to releasing the shackles that have bound you. Regardless of who else loves you, you can begin to give yourself that nurturing, and rebuild strength to face any battles ahead.

Once you have worked on self-doubt; you will experience self-acceptance and self-love.

You will never change the world by being just like it. Accept yourself as an individual.

Self-love has been repeatedly talked about over the years and has become an almost whimsical ideal used by thousands of coaches, writers, therapists and experts as the answer to all our problems. Now while that is true to a large extent and we can't "fill up another's cup when our own is empty" there isn't a magic formula or a handbook for what that means to you.

Acts of self-love and compassion are purely things that you include in your life, that bring a sense of pleasure and make you feel valued. They don't have to take three hours of your already stretched timetable or cost a lot of money. You don't have to earn them as a payoff for doing twice as much for other people.

Simple acts such as going to bed five minutes earlier, ditching the clothes in your wardrobe that make you feel frumpy, buying yourself a coffee and watching the world go by for fifteen minutes, or sitting outside your house briefly when you get home from work, and playing a track on your iPod that you love, before you go back to your chaotic household life, are all prime examples of things you can do to nurture yourself without too much effort.

Self-compassion is so interlinked with self-acceptance that they are almost conjoined twins. For every act of self-care you try to include in your life, if there are elements to yourself you don't accept you will never feel worthy of any self-love at all.

So, you need to work on them in unison. Acceptance is one of life's most challenging lessons to learn. It is a skill that needs to be mastered by repetitive practice. In the beginning, it can be so excruciating to even accept a compliment from someone, that you almost automatically counteract their words of appraisal.

Learn to say thank you, even if it is through gritted teeth at the start. In time you will be able to give genuine thanks for their kind words and may start to give yourself compliments too. I know I'm not alone in this struggle with receiving and being a people pleaser first, self-nurturer last.

So for those of you out there who feel the same; know that when someone gives you a gift, a compliment, a smile or a hug, it is an act of love and one you very much deserve just for being you, exactly as you are.

Be patient with yourself in the process. You are undoing years of self-hate and that's not an easy feat, but it's not an impossible task either.

Developing empathy

Beginning to develop a sense of empathy for others takes us away from a perspective of pain, judgement and victimhood, to one of compassion and courage. We learn to accept people as they are and accept ourselves more in the process.

It took a lot of counselling for me to realise that the abuse I had accepted from others had been as a result of their own suffering projected onto me.

Happy and content people don't treat other people with disrespect. We are all just repeating patterns that make sense within our map of the world, and sometimes these patterns aren't in alignment with the happiness of others too.

The experiences I had been through in relationships were as a result of their own pain taking over. Most of the people I had been with were all decent, good-hearted people, just lost in a world of confusion themselves.

Knowing this gave me the choice over what I wanted to do with that knowledge. I recognised that I had no control over another person’s actions, but also that they had no control over mine. I could decide what I would allow in my life and how I would respond to others.

This gave me a whole new perspective and I started to lose the need for acceptance from everyone, as well as the need to judge their lives in return.

I developed a sense of compassion for others, rather than distrust and fear. I could see that people only change when they are ready and if they really want to. I had witnessed that enough with myself. No matter what help and support I had received over the years, it was always down to me what I did with that guidance, and if I felt it served me better to be a victim or to act.

Learning to view life with empathy and understanding and letting go of the need to change the relationships I had with family, friends or partners to ones I’d yearned for, was liberating.

I understood that we all walk our different paths, with our own unique experiences. I understood suffering through my own eyes, but I could never see another person's suffering through their eyes. All I could do was support them and listen when they needed an ear.

It has never been my job to rescue them from their pain. I do not have all the answers. We are each responsible for our happiness and letting go of my ego and need to be needed was huge.

It’s a tough thing to admit but we are not here to save others, we are just here to live alongside them.

Autumns Lessons of Fulfilment & Relationships

That young woman was starting to let go of her past and
beginning to find her purpose.
Reflecting on all that had come before and all that was still to come.
Building on her strengths, facing new challenges and overcoming fears.
It was time to embrace life for all it had to offer,
away from monetary value, closer to core value.

Purpose

There is no financial value that can be put on the wealth you will feel when living with real purpose.

We can often put too much emphasis on money and forget about how our work makes us *feel*, how it benefits others and what impact it has on the world around us. When we live with intention and purpose, we approach our work from a different perspective. It becomes a joy and pleasure to create, serve and go out of our way to help others.

The money will flow to help support that intention, often in ways you wouldn't have imagined or accepted before. We just need to focus on the project ahead of us and allow ourselves to be driven more by our heart than our ego.

Our time on this earth is limited.

We have a choice to spend many of our years working hard to maintain a certain lifestyle, or we can find a balance by doing something that we love and adapting our life to the monetary gains that follow.

It is more than possible to have rich abundance and live out your dreams. It isn't a trade of one over the other, but it's important not to get lost in chasing the end financial rewards and missing the value of the journey to get there.

So how do you find your purpose?

By listening to what lights you up and by doing more of that.

Does sitting at an office desk eight hours a day light you up and fill you with excitement every morning?

Does working with children/elderly/disadvantaged adults sing to you?

Does working outdoors make you want to get up even earlier to get there?

Do you want to help people practically, emotionally or creatively?

What makes you feel more alive?

What inspires you?

What did you always dream of achieving or doing?

What legacy do you want to leave behind?

You don't have to leave your stable job and risk losing your house because of defaulting on the mortgage. You can transition slowly and add more value to your current timetable by including more of what you love in your day.

Volunteer at weekends for causes that mean something to you. Add to your hobbies. Make time for creativity in your life. Set goals for things you would like to achieve over the next five years and start implementing the steps to get there.

You will find your current job doesn't feel so exhausting and draining as you balance it out with things that bring value to your day. You may want to continue with that balance, or you may want to move away from work that doesn't fill you with as much joy. Either way, you are in the driver's seat of your life and you decide how much you want to live from purpose.

Let the Leaves Go

We all have resistance to letting certain things go. Certain beliefs, certain people or certain ambitions. It's not difficult to get caught up in ideas about how things 'should' be. It allows our brain to make sense of an otherwise chaotic world by bringing routine and a sense of normality.

Letting go would signify things changing, sometimes leaving us in unknown territory and threatening our sense of safety.

We habitually think a particular way for most of our lifetimes, so letting go of that and trying to believe in new ideas brings up doubt and scepticism.

What if I fail? What if I let people down? What if I fall flat on my face? What if people find out who I really am?

We do not expect the oldest trees in our forest to ever fall. We look to them for their knowledge and advice, and we see we are mere saplings in comparison.

When the mighty grow tired, and their bodies age, it reflects to us the need to use what we have to its fullest potential. We can't always have the energy of a child or the strength of a teenager, but our spirit remains strong and calls out for adventure. We just need to stop and listen.

Letting go and embracing life aren't difficult to do, but they can be difficult to sustain without dedication.

When someone leaves, we reminisce on all the good times, crave for them to come back, to reset the life as we know it, yet in the process we struggle to make the most of those we do have in our lives.

When we are faced with illness, we forget what things were like before and can easily get sucked into wallowing.

When our loved ones die, we acknowledge how short life can be for a brief time and are filled with enthusiasm to make the most of every day, then fall back into old patterns of the mundane.

Letting go of people is tough. Partly through a need to be accepted or liked by everyone, and partly through fear. Even toxic relationships can grow to be familiar. Letting them go can trigger guilt or a sense of failure for not being able to maintain the same level of connection, as if none of us evolve or grow. We feel ungrateful if we have been friends for decades, and now we're realising that we've grown apart.

It's easy to forget that some of your beliefs, for what success is in career, money or relationship terms, were formed decades ago, some of the people in your life - including family and friends you've known forever - are not on the same wavelength as you, and may well have different interests now, and some of the plans you had created were based on old ideals.

With this in mind, are we holding on to things for the right reason? Or is it time to start releasing the ties that bind us, despite the resistance?

I understand that it is easy for me to say, 'let it go'. The theme song will inevitably sing through your head even as you read the words. But it really can be that easy. It's all a matter of choice and taking small steps at a time.

You are not expected to just change your behaviours and belief systems overnight.

What beliefs still make sense to you and allow you to feel inspired, motivated and capable?

What did you always dream of achieving or doing?

What belief systems keep you feeling stuck, not good enough or incapable?

Begin to look at those negative beliefs and see if they still have any validity and start to replace them with more of the beliefs that lift you up instead.

Who still makes you feel uplifted when you are around them?

Who do you admire?

Who makes you feel drained or insecure?

Spend more time with those that lift you up and less time with those who are toxic to your spirit. Reach out to new people who have similar interests, nurture the areas of your life that fill you with joy and you will meet like-minded people that fit in with who you are now. In the present day.

As you begin to let go of things there will be mixed emotions that arise. Some feelings of relief, freedom and liberation, intertwined with feelings of fear, doubt and guilt. All are completely normal.

It is also normal to revert to old habits and beliefs occasionally or invite toxic people back into your life. It's almost like we must test ourselves that we really need to let them go. A reminder that, yes, we want something different.

Just go gentle on yourself in the process, because that's what it all is, a process, and processes don't happen overnight. Remember, trees don't shed their leaves overnight either.

Reflection

We are taught that being present is the ultimate way to live, but I believe that being able to reflect and look forward to plan where we want to be heading, is just as valuable occasionally.

It gives us a chance to adjust things and develop a sense of fulfilment in our achievements.

Self-reflection is often over-looked, and we just carry on with our little routines without question, never acknowledging how far we've come, or our unique qualities.

When we first begin to reflect on who we are, where we are in our lives and the choices we have made, it is easy to come from a place of judgement and self-criticism. We may struggle to be content with what we see and find it difficult to look at things objectively without guilt, sadness or regret. All too often we have higher expectations of ourselves than are realistic.

It takes practice to reflect on where you are with kind eyes and give yourself the encouragement and support that you would give to someone else that you love unconditionally. Beginning to love yourself, in the same way, can feel alien to most of us, but it is entirely possible over time.

Acknowledge a few things about yourself each day.

"I'm sorry for seeing your flaws before your beauty, for dumbing down what you wanted to say, for being a people pleaser".

"I forgive you for not being perfect, for not taking the steps to act in your best interests sooner, for listening to your inner critic more than your inner cheerleader".

"I'm grateful for being so raw and authentic, for you sharing your voice, for you challenging yourself"

"I love you for being so brave, for wanting to better yourself every day, for starting to practise self-care".

Just the act of finding things to appreciate or let go of brings you more into a state of power. You are more able to make informed decisions moving forward. You develop a sense of pride and self-worth and your motivation levels increase as you want to achieve things that you can reflect on with joy instead of regret.

Will you still shout at the kids when you're are running late? Yes

Will you still forget things? Yes

Will you still have moments of wanting to crawl back into bed and shut the world out? Yes

But will you also take more moments to breathe before you panic, anger or stress? Yes

Will you waffle on and offload a bit more? Hell yes!

Will you wake up with a bit less exhaustion before the day has even begun? Absolutely!

Without reflecting you may never see the amazing talents that you have to share or the value you have on this earth.

Winters Lessons of life without regret

That maturing woman sitting in stillness, looking back at her life and trying to see purpose within it all.
Beginning to stand tall despite the storms she was yet to face.
To live her truth and to move forward knowing each branch of her life had served a purpose and shaped her into what she had evolved into today.

Living Without Regret

Living life without regret is almost as difficult as living one without guilt, but both are necessary things to live a happier and more fulfilled existence.

We can spend so much time making plans and saying we will be happy when certain events happen or circumstances come together, that we forget that all we have is today. Putting off dreams for a later date runs you at risk of facing regret when you get to the later date and have still never managed to fulfil those dreams.

The only person who can chase those dreams is you. Nobody else can go out and grab them for you, so what are you waiting for?

We are intuitive beings, yet we can become blinded by the fears our minds have created over the years. At any moment we can take our control back and decide to face those fears, to create a happier life and to live it on our terms. It is up to us to take those small leaps of faith and push ourselves a bit more out of our comfort zone.

Life can be very simple, and often simplicity is key. We don't need to push for answers, we just need to let it flow.

Some of your life branches have been there for as long as you remember. They pretend to help, but actually hinder. They know exactly when you're feeling tired or haven't made yourself a priority and they cradle you with such a deep sense of security and comfort that you lose sight of your worries.

They are your bottle of wine at the end of the day to take the edge off, the coffee to stimulate you each morning to push through your body's tiredness, the working late and answering every text, so you feel you have value and importance.

They are the dieting, binging and purging to try and release the stress. They are the addiction to perfection and beauty that gives you a focus, but you never quite achieve. They are the cleaning rituals that cleanse out the confusion and they are the counting of likes, followers or shares that give you a sense of worth.

They have a death grip on you, and they aren't afraid to use it.

They have got you through some of the darkest times and now you feel like you owe them.

What if they were right all along? That you aren't strong enough, you aren't in control, you don't know what you need, you can't achieve anything meaningful without them, and you are nothing?

It takes a lot of practice and dedication to break these branches and begin habits that are from a place of self-care, not self-torture. But even if you can start to implement small changes, in time you will be free from their clutches.

Build yourself a support network and plan for the times you will need that support.

Take baby steps towards your health, and away from harm. Forgive yourself for not knowing better, or doing better before, and acknowledge your wins when you do make a better choice.

Anxiety Without Regret

Being able to walk with anxiety and knowing it is just a survival mechanism, not a cross to bear, gives you control back. You can choose how you listen to it and how you act upon it. There is power in that.

Anxiety can be less of an enemy and more of an alarm system to bring you back to the present.

It brings you smack bang, right back into your body, and provides you with overwhelming sensations that you can't ignore. It allows you to witness what is going on emotionally when otherwise you might have brushed over your concerns and worries.

If you can just stop and notice what it is trying to tell you, and stop trying to fight it, anxiety will happily walk along as your cloak, not your cloud.

Give yourself space to observe what the anxiety feels like in your body, and where it is.

What colour is it? What shape? What sound? What words are coming to mind?

Write down a description of it, give it a name, create a character to represent it, that sits on your shoulder or hides in your belly button. The more you can remind yourself that anxiety isn't who you are, but an experience you are going through, the less it will suffocate you and bury you when it strikes.

It's just a branch in the tree of life and the woods grow when we let them.

Relationships Without Regret

We are a world of around seven billion people, and despite us becoming more connected than ever through technology, we are becoming increasingly disconnected, with actual, real-time human interaction, with feelings of loneliness on the rise.

We have grown more fearful of being vulnerable or real with others and have lost the ability to have those conversations that create deeper relationships.

It feels like we have developed a greater fear of failure and rejection, because we're exposed to more criticism, via more people through social media, including complete strangers, or 'trolls.'

We have forgotten what authentic conversations look like because we are seeking followers and shares instead, and we have grown terrified of being judged.

But we are not defined by how many followers we have; how many likes a post gets or how amazing we look through filters.

We all crave a true human connection.

The ability to make each other laugh, share experiences, honour each other's fears and express gratitude for each other's gifts. We are tribal creatures and we want to feel that sense of being part of the clan, part of the forest.

Those things can't be gained through systems that are designed for instant gratification. The swipe-left culture, the perfect image, or the twitter feed. They require time away from screens, commitment and opening up.

When was the last time you left your phone at home and lived in the moment fully?

If you can't even remember a time, then it has been too long.

Try it more often and witness the effect that has.

Grab a coffee with a friend and truly listen to their words, go for a walk and see nature in her beauty, not through a screen capture, play on the swings with your children and tell someone exactly what they mean to you.

You may be surprised by the results.

For every facet of you, that you think will be rejected, there will be another person amongst the seven billion, that understands, and has been through similar. So, stop hiding away.

Confidence Without Regret

We see selfies all day every day, people posing with smiles and laughter, but is there real confidence behind those pearly whites, and what does confidence really look like anyway?

It is about feeling comfortable in your own skin and having a sense of self-acceptance of your imperfections.

Women, men and children go from hating themselves and hiding away from the world to embracing their flaws, and there's no disguising the light that shines out of their eyes as a result. That spark and energy oozes out of them and it's infectious and beautiful.

So how do we gain confidence?

It comes from having space and support to express your inner doubts, fears and insecurities without receiving criticism or advice, and through learning that it's ok to not be ok.

It comes from pushing yourself gradually out of your comfort zone and noticing that some of the limits you have placed on yourself aren't valid; that your value is not defined by your clothes size, your net worth or how many letters you have after your name; that you are so much more than that, with so much more to offer.

It's a constant learning curve and you may find yourself having several conversations in your head arguing with that inner critic.

If you could just be you, unapologetically raw, branches exposed, without facing rejection and disapproval, would you take the opportunity? How much lighter and free would you feel as a result?

Chase that dream, face that fear and dive headfirst into life for a while.

The more you challenge your limitations, the more you will want to try.

Reach out to people who are doing the things you would love to have the confidence to do. They started somewhere too, and most of the time they are more than happy to offer tips and tricks for you to do the same.

You were born to shine, so let yourself shine.

We can never be everything to everyone. We are not perfect. We are all just doing the best job we can with what we have.

Our life seasons teach us to play, create, seek out adventure, connect, grow, evolve, let go, rest, repair and heal. It is a never-ending cycle through the flow of the seasons, the budding spring, the blooming summer, the release of autumn and the stillness of the winter.

When we see our own cycles there is no question of if we are enough, because we are ever-changing and always enough.

Don't regret a thing.

Stand tall, roots exposed, branches wide in all your beautiful glory.

Authors Note

I never saw myself writing blogs, let alone books, despite it being a long-held dream. I have always written; diaries, letters to pen friends, ridiculously long rant texts to friends, but I never really considered that what I waffle on about might have any impact on others, until it started to.

I didn't envision that I would be able to overcome my struggles or to keep going despite having all the odds stacked against me. I never saw myself as achieving anything with my life full stop. I imagined I would just keep starting things, but never seeing them through to the end.

I have been wanting to write a book for most of my life, but because I have a brain like spaghetti junction with ideas whizzing along at 60mph I put it off repeatedly, not knowing where to start.

At some point though, I realised that when you don't know where to start you just need to start *somewhere.* So, I began to just type the words on the page.

I pushed myself out of my comfort zone hugely by putting personal stories out there for the whole world to see, I've stood in front of groups of women and spoke about techniques that have pulled me out of dark times, in the hope it might give them the boost to do the same, and I've started to put myself and my needs first.

My words are my legacy and the imprint and inspiration I want to leave behind. I write them for my children, I write them for my friends, and I write them for anyone who needs to know that they are not alone. For anyone who needs to know that we all have our trials in life, we all make choices that don't serve us well, we all have the ability to change and we can all write our own chapters.

Writing my book has been a deeply therapeutic experience that I hadn't even imagined possible. Reflecting on my life through script, identifying the roles I've played, the masks I have worn and the insecurities I have felt, in order to shape them into dialogue that made sense.

I played witness to myself and saw how I had started to shift my way of thinking through the seasons of my life and how my priorities began to change as a result.

I saw how I no longer wanted to drink, I changed my diet, I did more yoga and meditation, I started to learn new skills, I started to accept help and I learned to develop healthier boundaries.

I also saw how raw life can be, and how messy and real it all was when written in black and white. I questioned who would want to see that, until people started asking me the questions.

How did you overcome an eating disorder? Did you always know you would be an empowerment coach? How do you maintain a smile through the storms of life?

People were seeking the answers in order to act as a catalyst for their own transformation. Suddenly they didn't see achievements as being unattainable, because I'm no different from most people. I just have a fighting spirit that won't let me give in easily to defeat.

I strongly believe we all have that spark within us, and it just needs more oxygen and fuel to ignite.

If I can provide that for people by showing up for them, knowing that I haven't got it all sorted and there's still work to do, but that it's ok to be human and a work in progress, then that is one of the most empowering things I can do.

About the Author

Susanne created Tailored-Therapies Ltd after working as a holistic therapist for over a decade and finding that many clients were wanting increasingly more emotional support and guidance.

It is an organisation developed from a deep passion to give back and create space for others to find their own inner strength and power.

Tailored-Therapies is dedicated to helping others develop resilience, self-esteem, confidence and positive mental well-being habits.

Susanne runs a range of courses, workshops and one to one sessions to support individuals to develop these skills and to provide a community for them to learn and grow.

Susanne has worked along side several services supporting women escaping abuse, addiction & trauma and has seen the impact it can have on people's lives when they finally begin to understand and accept themselves.

If you'd like to learn more, find me at www.tailored-therapies.co.uk

Follow me on Instagram @living_empowered

Facebook @TailoredTherapiesLtd

Or join my private women's empowerment group: Empowerment Sistas.

Printed in Great Britain
by Amazon

30818798R00109